Gold in the Water

Shane O'Reilly

with **Paul Curley**

Music by Denis Clohe

I0203492

methuen | drama

LONDON · NEW YORK · OXFORD · NEW DELHI · SYDNEY

METHUEN DRAMA

Bloomsbury Publishing Plc, 50 Bedford Square, London, WC1B 3DP, UK
Bloomsbury Publishing Inc, 1359 Broadway, New York, NY 10018, USA
Bloomsbury Publishing Ireland, 29 Earlsfort Terrace, Dublin 2, D02 AY28, Ireland

BLOOMSBURY, METHUEN DRAMA and the Methuen
Drama logo are trademarks of Bloomsbury Publishing Plc

First published in Great Britain 2025

Cover design: Pete Reddy
Cover image © Ros Kavanagh

A catalogue record for this book is available from the British Library.

A catalog record for this book is available from the Library of Congress.

ISBN: PB: 978-1-3506-1711-7
         ePDF: 978-1-3506-1712-4
         eBook: 978-1-3506-1713-1

Series: Modern Plays

Typeset by Westchester Publishing Services

For product safety related questions contact productsafety@bloomsbury.com.

To find out more about our authors and books visit
www.bloomsbury.com and sign up for our newsletters.

Gold in the Water 2025 – One Thousand Pieces & Lovano

Book and Lyrics	**Shane O'Reilly**
Co-Writer	**Paul Curley**
Composer	**Denis Clohessy**
Director	**Ronan Phelan**
Choreography and Movement Direction	**Philip Connaughton**
Set Design	**Maree Kearns**
Costume Design	**Catherine Fay**
Lighting Design	**Sarah Jane Shiels**
Music Director	**Danny Forde**
Producer	**Pádraig Heneghan (Lovano)**
Producing Assistant	**Jack Shanley**
Production Manager	**Eamonn Fox**
Associate Production Manager	**Frank Commins**
Stage Manager	**Sophie Flynn**
Assistant Stage Manager	**Rachel Stout**
Costume Supervisor	**Nicola Burke**
Wardrobe Maintenance	**Jordan Kearns**

Cast

Pet Shelter Owner	**Clare Barrett**
Rosaleen/Cockatoo	**Ruth Berkeley**
Harvey	**Domhnall Herdman**
Bart	**Matthew Malone**
Deirdre/Mouse	**Niamh McAllister**
Tom/Terrapin	**Tiernan Messitt-Greene**
Sandra/Rabbit	**Rachel O'Byrne**

The original cast for *Gold in the Water* included Fiona Browne, Harley Cullen Walshe, Oliver Flitcroft, Kate Gilmore, Mark Keegan.

Creative Bios

SHANE O'REILLY Writer

Shane O'Reilly is an actor and a writer who lives in Dublin.

Shane's theatre writing includes: *Her Father's Voice* (LOVANO, Dublin Theatre Festival), *Gold in the Water* (LOVANO, Project Arts/National Tour); *swansong* (Barnstorm Theatre Company) *windowpane* (The Abbey Theatre – Dear Ireland); *The Water Boys* (Equinox Theatre); *FOLLOW, FARM, CARE* (co-created with WillFredd Theatre).

Shane has written and directed works for film that include *The Water Boys, PAL* and *Näher*.

PAUL CURLEY Co-writer

Paul Curley is a performer and theatre-maker with particular expertise in making theatre for young audiences. As an actor and collaborator he has worked with a wide range of companies in Ireland and the UK. Work includes: *Polar Bear & Penguin* (Paul Curley & John Currivan with Draíocht), *Night Light* (Teater Refleksion, Denmark), *White* (Catherine Wheels, Scotland), *Black Beauty* (Red Bridge Arts, Scotland), *The Bockety World of Henry & Bucket, A Murder of Crows, Song From The Sea, Jack, Boy with a Suitcase* (Barnstorm Theatre Company), *How to Keep an Alien* (Sonya Kelly & Rough Magic), *Care* and *Farm* (WillFredd Theatre), *Happily Ever After* (Action Transport Theatre), *Snow Mouse* (Travelling Light/The Egg), *An Ideal Husband* (The Gate Theatre), *Assassins* (Rough Magic SEEDS), *Mr Benn, Monster Hits* (Tall Stories, London), *Bonjour Bob* (Theatre Alibi), *Jack* (Tutti-Frutti). In collaboration with Designer Ger Clancy, Paul has created *Bake!, The Dig, Grey Matter* and *The Elephant in the Room*. Paul is a member of TYA Ireland and a participant of Meitheal CPS 2022-24. Originally from County Galway, Paul lives in Dublin with his husband and co-writer of *Gold in the Water*, Shane O'Reilly.

DENIS CLOHESSY Composer

Denis has previously worked with The Abbey Theatre, The Gate Theatre, Fishamble, Once Off Productions, Rough Magic, CoisCéim, Junk Ensemble, Northlight Theatre, Chicago and Beijing Children's Art Theatre. Denis was an associate artist with the Abbey in 2008 and was a participant on Rough Magic's ADVANCE programme in 2012.

Composition for Film and Television includes the feature films One Night In Millstreet Fastnet Films Older than Ireland Snack box Films, His and Hers Venom Film, The Irish Pub Atom Films and the animation series Will Sliney's Storytellers Fastnet Films. He won Irish Times theatre awards in 2011 and 2019 and was a nominee in 2015. He also won best score at the Underground Cinema awards in 2013 and the European short film *Biennale* in 2005.

RONAN PHELAN Director

Ronan Phelan is a Dublin-based theatre director whose work spans new writing, musical theatre, and reimagined classics. A former Associate Director of Rough Magic Theatre Company, he is known for productions that balance formal precision with freedom, wit, and emotional clarity.

For Rough Magic, Ronan directed *Much Ado About Nothing* (Irish Times Theatre Award nominee, Best Director 2020), *Glue, Tonic, A Portrait of the Artist as a Young Man*, and the Irish premiere of Lucy Prebble's *The Effect*. Other work includes Erica Murray's *The Loved Ones* (Gate Theatre / Dublin Theatre Festival), TKB's *It's Always Your Bleedin' Own* (Project Arts Centre), the original musical *Gold in the Water* by Shane O'Reilly with Paul Curley and Denis Clohessy (Project / Mermaid, national tour 2025), *All Mod Cons* (Lyric Theatre, Belfast), and *Annie* (Cork Opera House).

An alumnus of the Rough Magic SEEDS programme and former Resident Assistant Director at the Abbey Theatre, Ronan teaches regularly at The Lir Academy. His work is marked by generosity, craft, and a fascination with how performance exposes the structures – personal, political, and theatrical – through which we understand one another.

PHILIP CONNAUGHTON Choreographer and Movement Director

Philip Connaughton is a choreographer and performer from Dublin. He has presented his work nationally and internationally, collaborating across dance, theatre, opera, and the visual arts. In 2014 he founded Company Philip Connaughton and has since created works such as *Mortuus Est Philippus, Whack!!, Trojans, Assisted Solo, Mamafesta Memorialising*, and *Party Scene* (with THISISPOPBABY). Recent projects include *Yes, but do you care?* (with Marie Brett, commissioned by IMMA), *Trojans* (for Cork Midsummer Festival), *WAKE* (with THISISPOPBABY), and the short film *Rebellious Hope* (in collaboration with Luca Truffarelli), featuring a cast of extraordinary mature dancers with music by composer Mel Mercier.

MAREE KEARNS Set Designer

Maree's career in theatre design has led to her being a regular creative collaborator with many of Ireland's leading companies and directors in theatre, dance, opera and musicals. She has created worlds for performance on stages big and small across the country and internationally, in site-specific locations, immersive experiences and outdoor productions.

Recent work includes *Little Shop of Horrors* at the Bord Gais Energy Theatre, *Our New Girl* at the Lyric Theatre, Belfast; *The Black Wolfe Tone* (Irish Repertory Theatre, New York and Fishamble); *Sive* at the Gaiety Theatre, *Hammam* by Añu Productions & *Somewhere Out there You* at the Abbey Theatre.

Maree's has designed for The Abbey Theatre, The Ark, Anu Productions, The Bord Gais Energy Theatre, Everyman Theatre, Fishamble Theatre Company, CoisCeim Dance Theatre Company, Cork Opera House, Corn Exchange, Gaiety Productions, Landmark Productions, The Lyric and many more.

Maree has also worked extensively in television and film and is the course director for the MFA in Theatre Design at the Lir Academy in Dublin. She has had multiple nominations and won the Irish Times Theatre award for Set Design and was the recipient of the Tanya Moiseiwitsch design award at the Tyrone Guthrie Centre in 2024.

For more information see www.mareekearns.com

CATHERINE FAY Costume Designer

Catherine Fay is an award-winning Costume Designer from Tallaght, Dublin, working across Theatre, Dance and Opera. She has an MFA in Art in the Contemporary World from NCAD.

In her practice, she uses methods of disassembling to investigate connection. Her many credits include *The Crucible* (West End/National Theatre), *Emma, Grania, The Quare Fellow, Somewhere Out There You, Translations, Portia Coughlan* (Abbey Theatre), *Piaf, Romeo and Juliet* and *The Threepenny Opera* (Irish Times Theatre Award nomination) (Gate Theatre, Dublin), *Madam Butterfly, MARS, Die Fledermaus, Giulio Cesare, Elektra* and *Orfeo and Euridice* (INO), *The Plough and the Stars* (Abbey Theatre/Lyric Hammersmith), *The United States vs. Ulysses* (Pavilion/Irish Arts Centre, NYC), *A Midsummer Night's Dream* and *Handel's Giulio Cesare* (BVOF), *Making History* and *Gatman!* (Everyman Cork/Project Arts Centre), *Gold in the Water* (Project Art Centre/Mermaid), *Outrage, Embargo* and *The Treaty* (Fishamble), *Breaking Dad* (Landmark Productions), *GLUE* (Rough Magic), *Näher . . . nearer, closer, sooner, 12 Minute Dances, Totems* (Liz Roche Company), *The Return of Ulysses, Owen Wingrave, Semele* (Opera Collective Ireland), *Acis and Galatea* (Opera Theatre Company), *The Importance of Nothing* (Pan Theatre Company), *Owen Wingrave* (Opera Bastille, Paris), *Girl Song* and *Dogs* (United Fall).

SARAH JANE SHIELS Lighting Designer

Sarah Jane is a lighting designer, whose interest in light began as a member of Dublin Youth Theatre. She collaborates with a diverse range of companies, working in theatre, dance, opera and installation.

Upcoming productions include *Dénouement* (Lyric Theatre Belfast), *Cunning Little Vixen* (Irish National Opera) and *The Mirror Stage* (Brokentalkers).

Recent productions include *Octopus Children* (THISISPOPBABY at Dublin Fringe Festival), *L'elisir d'amore* (Irish National Opera), *Our New Girl* (Lyric Theatre Belfast), *The Borrowers* (Gate Theatre).

She has a BA in Drama and Theatre Studies and a M.Sc in Interactive Digital Media from Trinity College Dublin. She was a participant on the Rough Magic Seeds programme and co-founder of WillFredd Theatre and the Irish Society of Performance Designers.

DANNY FORDE Music Director

Danny Forde is a composer, singer-songwriter, music director and multi-instrumentalist from Dublin. His composition work includes feature film *The Apprentice* (2024), *Medea/Jason* (Setagaya Public Theatre Tokyo), and *The Maker* (Dan Colley). His work as music director includes the productions *The Dead* (ANU/Landmark), *The Ferryman* (Gaiety Theatre), and new musical *Gold In The Water*.

Danny performs under the name Every Thing The Light Touches and has released a record of original songs. He has worked with a diverse array of artists including Loah, Bill Whelan, Anaïs Mitchell, FELISPEAKS, Discovery Gospel Choir and the Hothouse Flowers.

PÁDRAIG HENEGHAN, LOVANO Producer

Lovano is the producing entity for Pádraig Heneghan, one of Ireland's most experienced producers and general managers in the performing arts. Since 2012, he has worked with some of Ireland's leading independent artists in creating new work. He is currently working with Shane O'Reilly (*Gold in the Water* (2023) and upcoming Irish tour) and Jean Butler (*What We Hold* – 2022 Dublin Theatre Festival and 2024 – Irish Arts Centre, New York) and previously with Emma Martin/ United Fall and Michael Keegan-Dolan.

In 2022, Lovano co-produced *Walking with Ghosts*, written by and starring Gabriel Byrne, with Landmark Productions, in Dublin, Wexford and Broadway. Other work with Landmark includes *Backwards up a Rainbow* (Rosaleen Linehan and Conor Linehan, 2021) and generally managed the three summer seasons of a new production of *Once* at the Olympia Theatre (2015 – 2017). He is currently managing *The Weir* in Dublin for Landmark and Kate Horton Productions. He generally managed projects for Riverdream Productions (*Heartbeat of Home* – its world premiere and international touring (2013-2019)) and large-scale projects for Tyrone Productions in Croke Park.

Previously, he was Deputy Director at the Gate Theatre, Dublin and oversaw its touring to leading international festivals (Edinburgh, London, Sydney and New York) and transfers of its work to the West End and Broadway.

JACK SHANLEY Producing Assistant

Jack Shanley is a producer and stage manager from Dublin, and is a graduand of the Lir Academy's inaugural MFA in Theatre Producing, having previously studied at Trinity College Dublin and Inchicore College of Further Education.

Most recently, Jack has worked on the producing teams for *Reunion* (The Kiln Theatre, London), *The Weir* (3Olympia Theatre, Dublin, and Harold Pinter Theatre, London), *Krapp's Last Tape* (Pavilion Theatre, Dublin) with Landmark Productions, and is currently Producing Assistant on *Gold in the Water* (national tour) with One Thousand Pieces and Lovano.

As a stage manager, Jack has worked with Breda Cashe Productions, Pat Moylan Productions, Four Rivers Theatre Company, The Gate Theatre, Gift Horse Theatre, LemonSoap Productions, bluehouse theatre, Broad Strokes, Dublin Theatre Festival and Dublin Fringe Festival.

Upcoming producing credits include Breda Cashe Productions' *Cosima* (Bewley's Café Theatre, Dublin) and Landmark Productions and ANU's *The Dead* (Museum of Literature, Dublin).

SOPHIE FLYNN Stage Manager

Sophie has nearly 20 years of hands-on experience in stage management. She has had the privilege of working with all the major theatre companies in Ireland, managing everything from large-scale national tours to intimate, site-specific performances. Sophie is based in Dublin but has travelled extensively with work throughout her career.

Her stage managing credits include:

Macbeth/Riders double bill, Druid O Casey, Three Short Comedies, The Seagull, Druid Gregory, Cherry Orchard, The Beacon, Epiphany,

Richard III, King Of The Castle, Beauty Queen of Leenane (Druid) Dancing at Lughnasa, The President, New Electric Ballroom, The Steward of Christendom, The Heiress, Who's Afraid of Virginia Woolf, Pride and Prejudice, An Ideal Husband, The Threepenny Opera, Enemy of The People, Krapps Last Tape (The Gate Theatre) *The Approach, The First Child, Medicine, Grief Is The Thing With Feathers, Happy Days, Postcards from the Ledge, Arlington, Once, Ballyturk, Breaking Dad, Talk of The Town, The Second Violinist* (Landmark) *Trad, The Dead School* (Livin Dred) *Translations* (National Theatre) *Outrage* (Fishamble)

Her film and television credits include *Gilgamesh* (Macnas), *St Patrick's Day Parade '19, Dancing With The Stars* (Shinawil), *Play Next Door* (VIP), *Lunasa* (RTE), *Obama Concert, College Green* (MCD), *Magners League Awards, Vodafone GAA Awards, Take Me Out, The Childline Concert, IFTA Awards* (Observe), *Deal or no Deal* (Endamol Productions), *The All Ireland Talent Show* (Tyrone Productions).

RACHEL STOUT Assistant Stage Manager

Rachel is a Galway based stage manager, her passion for the arts was sparked from a young age. She studied performing arts and has previously worked in lighting and costume.

Her assistant stage management credits include *Macbeth*, *Riders to the Sea*, *Three Short Comedies*, *The House*, *Shadow of Gunman*, *Druid: O'Casey*, *The Last Return*, *The Seagull*, *Druid:Gregory* (Druid), *Outrage* (Fishamble), *Cnamha la Loba*, *Danse Macabre*, *Symphony for the Restless*, *This Thunderous Heart* (Macnas)

She has stage managed *Wild Swimming* (Alisha Finnerty), *Mr. Bergmann of Deadman's Point*, *The Middle of Somewhere*, *The Words are There* (Nth degree), *Snapshot*, *Compostela* (Miriam Needham), *A Galway Girl* (3 rings).

Cast Bios

CLARE BARRETT Pet Shelter Owner

Clare graduated with distinction from the Conservatoire at T.U. Dublin (formerly D.I.T.) in 2003. Since then she has worked with many theatre companies performing both in Ireland and internationally.

Recent theatre credits include: *The United States Versus Ulysses* (Irish Arts Centre/Once Off Productions), *Emma* (Abbey Theatre), *The Shadow of a Gunman* (Druid Theatre Company/National Tour), *The Quare Fella* (Abbey Theatre), *Every Brilliant Thing* (Decadent Theatre Company/Galway International Arts Festival), *Gold in the Water* (One Thousand Pieces & Lovano – Project Arts Centre/ Mermaid), *Medicine* (Landmark – Edinburgh International Festival, Galway International Arts Festival, St. Ann's Warehouse NYC), *Wild Horses* (Fishamble), *Trad* (Livin Dred – National Tour), *Much Ado About Nothing* (Rough Magic – Kilkenny Arts Festival/National tour) – Nominated for Best Supporting Actress Irish Times Theatre awards, *The Unmanageable Sisters* (Abbey Theatre), *Wizard of Oz* (Cork Opera House), *Minding Frankie* (Lowry Theatre/Gaiety Theatre/National tour), *Angela's Ashes* (LimeTree Theatre/Bord Gais/ GOH Belfast), *The Train* (Rough Magic-Abbey Theatre/DTF/MAC) – nominated for Best Supporting Actress in the Irish Times Theatre Awards, *The Dead* (Performance Corporation – Project/National Tour), *Big Maggie* (Druid – Gaiety Theatre), *DruidShakespeare* (Druid National Tour/Lincoln Festival NYC), *Moll* (Verdant-Gaiety Theatre), I♥ALICE♥I (HotForTheatre – DFF/DTF/Peacock Theatre/World Tour/ National tour – Winner of Best Female Performer in the Absolut Fringe Festival.

Recent Film/TV includes: *The Lost Children of Tuam* (El Paso productions/Big Red Films/Element Pictures), *Only Child* – Series 1 & 2 (BBC 1/Happy Tramp North), *Fréwaka* (Doubleband productions), *Good Grief* (Netflix), *Sisters* (Sare & Suze Productions), *Wild Mountain Thyme* (Heather Productions), *The Last Right* (Deadpan/CrossDay), *The Flag* (Centenary Films), *Run and Jump* (Samson pictures). She also played Bronagh in RTÉ's *Fair City*.

RUTH BERKELEY   Rosaleen/Cockatoo

Ruth trained at Laine Theatre Arts with a degree in Musical Theatre. Some credits include: 'Mother/Moo' in *Dream Factory* (Dublin Theatre Festival), *Disenchanted* (Disney Live Action), 'Onna Crow', *A Man Of No Importance* (West End), 'God I Hope I Get It' (Fishamble Theatre, Company New Writers (BTP)), 'Power Woman' in *Menopause The Musical* (UK & IRE Tours), 'Lisa' in *Mamma Mia!* (International), *Vikings: Valhalla* (Netflix), Soloist in Cork Proms (Cork Opera House), Soloist in Andrew Lloyd Webber Experience (Richmond Theatre), 'Mistress/Nurse' in Brian Byrne's *Angel of Broadway* (NCH), Fairy in *Crossroads Pantomime's* (Grand Opera House, Belfast), 'Mary O'Brien' *Wishin & Hopin'* (Guildhall Theatre), 'Sophie/Mrs Greer' *Annie* (Cork Opera House), 'Gretchen the Witch' in *Hansel & Gretel* (The Mill, Bualadh Bos Children's Festival), Dance Captain/Ensemble for *The Mikado* (Lyric Opera NCH), 'US Glinda/Ensemble' in *The Wizard Of Oz* (Cork Opera House), 'Maleficent' in *Sleeping Beauty* (UCL), *Penny Dreadful* (Sky Atlantic), Soloist in A *Night At The Musicals* (Queens Theatre). Ruth is delighted to be a part of *Gold In The Water*.

DOHMNALL HERDMAN Harvey

Domhnall Herdman is a Belfast born actor and graduate of the Lir academy his most recent theatre credits include 'Tom Hanly' in *What Are You Afraid Of* with Rough Magic for DTF and 'Frank Churchill/ Mr Elton' in *Emma* at the Abbey Theatre. Some of his other credits include 'Gabriel' in *The Cyclone Kid*, 'Malachy Jnr' in *Angela's Ashes* (Pat Moylan Productions),and 'Jimmy' in *Faultline* with ANU.

On screen he has appeared as 'Liam O'Hagan' in *Borderline* for ITV, *The Doll Factory* (Paramount), 'Mark' in *A Few Can See* (Frank Sweeney), 'Jimmy' in *Idiot Fish* (BOBI LUX/Hakim Mao), 'Matt' in *Normal People*, and 'Biter' in RTÉ's *Smother*.

MATTHEW MALONE Bart

Matthew is an actor from Dublin. Named as one of The Irish Times' 50 people to watch, he has worked with many of Ireland's leading theatre companies, and recently played Alceste in *A Misanthrope*

(Sugarglass | Smock Alley). Matthew has been nominated by the Irish Times Irish Theatre Awards three times, including for the role of Bernard in Philip McMahon's *Once Before I Go* (Gate Theatre). Selected stage credits include *BREAKING*, *Embargo* (Fishamble), *An Old Song Half Forgotten* opposite Bryan Murray (Abbey Theatre), *The Boy Who Never Was* (Brokentalkers), *Tarry Flynn* (Livin' Dred), and *Faultline* (ANÚ | Gate Theatre). Screen credits include *Tall Tales & Murder* (BBC), *Romance is Dad* (Glenside), *The Rainmaker* (USA), *Few Can See*, *Dad* (RTÉ), *Miss Scarlet and The Duke* (PBS), *Valhalla* (Netflix), *The Resistance Fighter*, *Darkey Kelly* and *As Luck Would Have It*.

NIAMH MCALLISTER Deirdre/Mouse

Niamh is from Bangor, County Down. She received her BA in Acting from The Lir.

Theatre credits include *What Are you Afraid Of?* (Rough Magic & Kilkenny Arts Festival), *Fancy Dan* (Townhall Longford), *Made From Paper* (Mermaid Theatre), *Yerma* (Tinderbox Theatre Company at Lyric Theatre), *The Making of Mollie* (The Ark), *The Hen Do* (GBL Prod), *Romeo and Juliet* (The Mill Theatre), *New Fish* (Smock Alley Theatre) & *Blackout* (Lyric Theatre).

Niamh's film and TV credits include the upcoming feature film *Chasing Millions* which was directed by Stephen Burke, the TV series *Three Families* (BBC 1), and the feature film *Nocebo* directed by Lorcan Finnegan opposite Eva Greene.

Niamh also wrote and directed her first comedy short film *Dead on Arrival* for which she won the Best Emerging Irish Female Director Award at IndieCork in 2024. She is a member of the all-female comedy improv troupe 'Broad Strokes' who won the Spirit of Wit Award in Dublin Fringe Festival 2024 for their improvised business conference show *B.S Incorporated.*

TIERNAN MESSITT-GREENE Tom/Terrapin

From Wexford, Tiernan has most recently been seen as Darragh in the short film *THE KNIFE* for Virgin Media, directed by Joy Nesbitt at Keeper Pictures, and on stage as Tony in Billy Walsh's

A Handful of Stars for Four Rivers Theatre Co., directed by Conall Morrison.

His recent screen credits include the role of Mark opposite Aoife Hinds in the short film *Swedish Death*, directed by Kristina Yee, Charlie in *A Merry Scottish Christmas* directed by Dustin Rikert, Noah Henderson alongside Jane Seymour in the TV series *Harry Wild* directed by Ronan and Rob Burke, and Rory in Claire Niererpraum's feature *Lucky in Love* alongside Allen Leech. On stage Tiernan played the role of Hamlet in *Hamlet* for the Mill Theatre, directed by Katie O'Halloran.

Tiernan also recently played the role of Ted in Billy Roche's *The Cavalcaders*, directed by Aaron Monaghan for Druid Theatre Company, and the part of Ray alongside Marion O'Dwyer, Mark Fitzgerald and Sarah Madigan in *The Beauty Queen of Leenane* directed by Ben Barnes.

RACHEL O'BYRNE Sandra/Rabbit

From Dublin, Rachel was in the first graduating class of the Bachelor in Acting program at The Lir Academy (2014).

Rachel was most recently seen in Druid's 50th anniversary production of *Macbeth & Riders to the Sea* (The Mick Lally Theatre & The Gaiety Theatre) and in Druid's *The House* (Town Hall Theatre, Galway & The Gaiety Theatre).

Rachel's other theatre credits include *Gold in The Water* (Project Arts/Mermaid), *Blackwater Lightship* (Gaiety Theatre), *The Long Christmas Dinner, The Remains of Maisie Duggan* and *By The Bog Of Cats* (Abbey Theatre), *The Dead* (Gaiety Theatre), *The Alternative* (Fishamble), *The Mai* (Decadent Theatre Company), *At The Ford* (Rise Productions), *The Great Gatsby, Assassins, A Christmas Carol, One For The Road* and *The Constant Wife* (The Gate Theatre, Dublin). She was nominated for an Irish Times Theatre Award for her performance in *These Stupid Things* (Smock Alley) by Hugh Travers in 2019.

On screen Rachel can be seen in *Mammal*, a feature by Rebecca Daly and in *Redemption* (C5/Virgin Media One).

Gold in the Water

Shane O'Reilly
with **Paul Curley**

Music by Denis Clohessy

Characters

Bart
Harvey, Bart's husband.
Sandra, Bart's best friend.
Tom, Sandra's husband.
Deirdre, Harvey's best friend.
Rosaleen, Bart's mother.
Pet Shelter Owner (PSO)

A Cockatoo
A Rabbit
A Terrapin
A Mouse

Babies and offstage voices to be sung by cast as appropriate.

Songs

 1. Something New.   Cockatoo
 2. Fabulous!   Full Cast
 3. Everything I've Ever Wanted.   Bart & Harvey
 4. At It Like Rabbits.   Rabbit & Pets
 5. Pet'Ernal Love.   PSO & Pets
 6. Fishy Feelings.   Bart & Harvey
 7. Sleep Baby Sleep.   Sandra, Tom, Bart
 8. Asking for a Friend.   Deirdre & Harvey
 9. Pick Me!   Terrapin
10. Careless People.   PSO, Bart & Harvey
11. The Little Things.   Bart & Rosaleen
12. Manic Mouse.   Mouse & Pets
13. Never Quite Alone.   PSO & Pets
14. Asking for a Friend (*reprise*).   Deirdre & Harvey
15. Come Back. Come Home.   Bart & Harvey & Full Cast
16. Don't Give Up!   Full Cast
17. Start Again.   Full Cast

For Emma

Prologue

A **Cockatoo** *enters.*

Song. Something New.

Cockatoo
HI
I'M A COCKATOO
WITH A VERY TINY
LITTLE BRAIN
IT'S WALNUT - SIZED
TO BE CLEAR
AND SO ALL I CAN
ACTUALLY DO
IS REPEAT THE THINGS
REPEAT THE THINGS
REPEAT THE THINGS
REPEAT THE THINGS
REPEAT THE THINGS
REPEAT THE THINGS
I HEAR

I HEAR THAT PEOPLE HAVE
BIG BRAINS
TO
ALTER THINGS
CHANGE UP THE THINGS
SWITCH OUT THE THINGS
RENEW THE THINGS
THEY DO

BUT CHANGE IS VERY DIFFICULT
YOU SEE
IT'S NOT EASY TO
SAY SOMETHING NEW
BE SOMETHING NEW
SEE SOMETHING NEW

DO SOMETHING NEW
IT'S HARD TO DO

SO WHEN SOMETHING NEW
FROM OUT OF THE BLUE
LANDS RIGHT IN ON YOU
WELL
WHAT DO YOU DO?
DO YOU REPEAT THE THINGS
THAT YOU ALWAYS DO
OR IS IT TIME
FOR SOMETHING NEW?

Act 1

Scene 1

Bart and **Harvey**'s *home. They are preparing a party to celebrate their first wedding anniversary.*

Song. Fabulous!

All   FABULOUS
                             TIME TO PARTY!

Bart   Harvey?

Harvey   Yes Bart?

Bart   Fetch the punch bowl.

Harvey   The special occasions punch bowl?

Bart   Exactly! This is an extremely special occasion.

Harvey   Can you believe it's been a year?

Bart   Time flies –

Both   – when you're in love!

They kiss.

All   FABULOUS
                             LOVE TO PARTY

Tom and **Sandra**, *each holding two of their four babies, leaving* **Bart** and **Harvey** *a voice message.*

Bart Voice Message   Hi, it's Bart, please leave a message and a compliment.

Tom   Hi Bob.

Sandra   It's Bart!

Tom   Bart! Sorry, baby brain! Tom here. Happy wedding anniversary, fair play to you. We're leaving now, just need to wait for our babysitter to stop hyperventilating. She wasn't expecting quadruplets.

Sandra   And neither were we!

They chuckle maniacally.

Tom   Sandra has some news for you.

Sandra   News . . . no!

Tom   Bart, Sandra and I are –

All   FABULOUS
                           LET'S GO PARTY
                           WITH OUR FRIENDS
                           BART AND HARVEY.

Rosaleen *leaving a voice message.*

Harvey Voice Message   Hi, it's Harvey. Leave a message – wait, is this record–

Rosaleen   Hi Harvey. It's your mother-in-law, just the person every man wants to hear from. I remember my first wedding anniversary, and then I have a drink, and I forget it. Mine's a white wine, cold. See you soon!

All   FABULOUS.

Deirdre *leaving a message.*

Bart and Harvey Old Landline   Hi, this is Bart and Harvey's old landline. We don't check these messages anymore, please call us on our mobile phones.

Deirdre   Hi Bart, hi Harvey. It's Deirdre! Happy wedding anniversary! Woooooo! I'm still at work. The birthday boy superglued his face to my foot. I'm fine, the kid might have a little scar. Anyway! I'm gonna be late.

All   FABULOUS.

Bart   I love this bunting!

Harvey   You are going all out.

Bart   Absolutely. Hold it higher!

Harvey   I love seeing you like this.

Bart   Stretch it out a bit, don't let it sag.

Harvey   All fun and sparkly.

Bart   Harvey, focus on the bunting.

Harvey   How can I focus on anything else but you!

Bart   You are stupidly sweet sometimes. Okay, checklist.

Harvey   Go!

Bart   Drinks.

Harvey   In the bowl!

Bart   Canapés.

Harvey   On the trays.

Bart   Decorations.

Harvey   Colourful yet classy!

Bart   Outfits.

Harvey (*a twirl*)   Fabulous.

Both   They're here!

All   FA FA FABULOUS,
                     SO SO FA FABULOUS
                     LIFE'S SO PERFECT WHEN,
                     WE'RE WITH OUR GORGEOUS
                     FRIENDS!

                     LIVE LIFE FULL OF FLAIR
                     LIVE LIFE WITHOUT A CARE
                     HERE'S TO ALL OF US
                     LET'S HAVE A FABULOUS

> PARTY, WHAT A PARTY
> BART AND HARVEY
> YOU ARE FABULOUS!
>
> PARTY, WHAT A PARTY
> BART AND HARVEY
> DON'T YOU CHANGE ON US!

Sandra *finds* **Bart**.

Sandra   Well hello there bestie!

Bart   Bestie? That's a throwback.

Tom *intercepts and hands a gift to* **Bart**.

Tom   Happy anniversary!

Bart   Oh! You didn't need to do that, I know how busy you both are.

Tom   It's that photo of you two when you were teenagers.

Bart   Aw!

Bart & Sandra (*Doing some naff routine*)   Best friends then, best friends now, best friends always.

Bart   Some things never change.

Tom   It was hanging in our hallway. We thought you'd like to have it because / we –

Sandra   . . . didn't have time to go shopping for gifts.

Both   We have quadruplets!

Harvey *brings* **Rosaleen** *a glass of wine*.

Harvey   Your glass of wine, as ordered.

Rosaleen   Oh, aren't you delightful. Tell me, Harvey, what do you do to forget?

Harvey   Oh, that's easy. I just don't remember in the first place.

Bart *cuts in*.

Bart Good evening Mother.

Rosaleen Don't call me Mother, it sounds ungrateful.

Bart What would you like me to call you?

Rosaleen Rosaleen.

Bart So affectionate.

Rosaleen I didn't bring a gift, I brought advice.

Bart Advice, everyone's favourite gift.

Rosaleen An unfortunate truth of life is that we all turn into our parents in the end. Don't end up like your father.

All   FA FA FABULOUS,
                    SO SO FA FABULOUS
                    LIFE'S SO PERFECT WHEN,
                    WE'RE WITH OUR GORGEOUS
                    FRIENDS!

                    LIVE LIFE FULL OF FLAIR!
                    LIVE LIFE WITHOUT A CARE
                    HERE'S TO ALL OF US
                    LET'S HAVE A FABULOUS

Tom I'm a fish and chips man but these little circle yokes are

All   FA-BU-LOUS

Sandra This is my first blow-dry in six months, I feel

All   FA-BU-LOUS

Rosaleen Ah, the first wedding anniversary! After this it's all –

All   FA-BU . . .

Deirdre *arrives with aplomb, dressed as a carrot.*

All Deirdre!

Deirdre Happy anniversary!

Rosaleen Is that woman dressed as a vegetable?

Deirdre I'm a honey roast carrot.

Bart Deirdre's a children's entertainer.

Deirdre   I've come straight from working a kid's birthday party. The child's vegan, so I opened with a vegetable monologue, knocked them for six with my artichoke shuffle and ended with my peas de resistance! (*She pulls out three peas and juggles them badly.*)

All   FA-BU-LOUS

Sandra *ting-ting-ting a glass. Everyone gathers around.*

Harvey   Oooh! A toast!

Sandra   ONE YEAR TODAY
                           WE SAID HURRAY
                           TO OUR BEST FRIENDS BART
                           AND HARVEY

Tom   I DUSTED OFF MY
                           OLD BLACK TIE
                           FOR A ROCKING WEDDING
                           PARTY

All   HERE! HERE!

Sandra   BART SAID I DO

Deirdre   AND HARVEY DID TOO

Sandra   THE TWO BECAME UNITED
                           SO RAISE YOUR GLASSES HIGH
                           LET'S TOAST THEM TONIGHT

All   DON'T CHANGE

Bart   THANK YOU, GUYS
                           WE WON'T CHANGE
                           IN FACT WE AIM TO STAY THE
                           SAME

Harvey   WE MIGHT CHANGE

Bart   OH NO WE WON'T
                           HELP ME TRY
                           AND SAY THIS RIGHT

Both

ALL OF YOU
ARE FAMILY
WITHOUT YOU
WE'RE INCOMPLETE

All

SPEECHES OVER
TIME TO PLAY
LET'S GET LOOSE
AND CELEBRATE
WITH DANCING
DANCING
PARTY
WHAT A PARTY
BART AND HARVEY
YOU ARE FABULOUS!
PARTY
LIFE'S A PARTY
BART AND HARVEY
DON'T YOU CHANGE ON US!
TIME TO GO FOR ALL OF US
WHAT A PARTY
FABULOUS!
DON'T YOU TWO GO CHANGE
ON US
BART AND HARVEY
WE THINK YOU ARE
FABULOUS
FA-BU-LOUS
FA-BU-LOUS
FA-BU-LOUS
FAAAA-BUUUUUU-LOUS

Scene 2

Bart *and* **Harvey** *are alone in the hum of the aftermath of the party.*

Harvey   What a night.

Bart   What a party!

Harvey   And now that everyone is gone we get to do our second favourite pastime.

Both   Cleaning the house!

Bart   Hey, happy anniversary Harvey.

Harvey   Aw.

                                   Song. Everything I've Ever Wanted.

Bart   THAT VERY FIRST DAY
                                   THAT I MET YOU
                                   WELL, I ALMOST RAN A MILE

Harvey   Bart?

Bart   YOU KNOCKED OVER STUFF
                                   YOU WERE IMPULSIVE
                                   YOU WERE TOTALLY
                                   NOT MY STYLE

Harvey   What's going on?

Bart   NOW, YOU SIGH WHEN I READ
                                   LATE AT NIGHT IN BED
                                   COZ YOU'D RATHER PLAY
                                   FOOTSIE INSTEAD
                                   YOU BREAK MY THINGS
                                   AND HOPE THAT I DON'T SEE
                                   SING OUT LOUD INSUFFERABLY
                                   AND THERE IS NOTHING
                                   I WOULD CHANGE ABOUT YOU
                                   AT ALL
                                   YOU'RE EVERYTHING I'VE EVER
                                   WANTED

YOU'RE EVERYTHING TO ME
YOU'RE EVERYTHING I'VE EVER
WANTED
EVEN IF YOU ARE
A LITTLE DITSY

Harvey   Thanks!

Harvey   YOU MUTTER AND TUT WHEN
I WANT TO BE SILLY
YOU HAVE TO BE IN CONTROL
YOU FIND IT HARD TO RELAX
PLAY PRETEND AND KICK BACK
YOU'RE SO SCARED TO HAVE
SOME FUN!

Bart   I'm having loads of fun.

Harvey   AND THERE IS NOTHING
I WOULD CHANGE ABOUT YOU
AT ALL
YOU'RE EVERYTHING I'VE EVER
WANTED
YES, YOU'RE EVERYTHING TO ME

Both   YOU'RE EVERYTHING I'VE EVER
WANTED

Harvey   EVEN IF YOU CAN BE
A CONTROL FREAK

Bart   OH YOU
REALLY KNOW HOW TO TICKLE
ME

Harvey   IT'S BECAUSE I'M SO FUNNY AND
SMART

Bart   OH I'M FULLY AWARE OF HOW
SMART YOU ARE

Harvey   IN MY OWN SPECIAL WAY!

Bart	AND YOU SCARE ME THE MOST OUT OF EVERYONE
Harvey	AND YOU KIND OF MAKE ME FEEL UNSURE
Bart	EVEN WHEN I'M ENTIRELY UNDONE BY YOU
Both	YOU LIGHT UP MY DAYS YOU'RE EVERYTHING I'VE EVER WANTED

Harvey   This is all so exciting, and to think this is just the beginning.

Bart   Yes.

Harvey   What's next for us, Bart?

Bart	THE THING THAT I WANT MORE THAN ANYTHING ELSE IS FOR NOTHING TO CHANGE AT ALL FOR JUST YOU AND ME TO STAY THE SAME IS EVERYTHING I NEED
Both	YOU'RE EVERYTHING I'VE EVER WANTED YOU'RE EVERYTHING TO ME YOU'RE EVERYTHING I'VE EVER WANTED EVERYTHING YOU AND ME

Bart   Let's leave the cleaning to the morning.

Harvey   Good idea.

Bart   Something to look forward to.

They kiss, and head off to bed. And while they sleep, a **Goldfish** *arrives out of the cosmos and lands on their doorstep.*

Scene 3

The following morning **Bart** *is taking out the rubbish from the party. He spots the* **Goldfish**.

Bart   Harvey?

Harvey   (**Harvey** *joins him*) Yes Bart? Oh, what's that?

Bart   It's a goldfish.

Harvey   A goldfish, wow! Where did it come from?

Bart   Out of the blue.

Harvey   That's so strange. I've heard of it raining cats and dogs but never goldfish. What will we do?

Bart   Flush it?

Harvey   Bart!

Bart   Joking. That was a joke.

Harvey *picks up the* **Goldfish**.

Harvey   Look at its little face. It looks scared.

Bart   Don't be silly, goldfish don't have feelings. They have a three-second memory. That fish has forgotten that you picked it up.

Harvey   How did it get here? On our doorstep.

Bart   No one else has a goldfish on their doorstep.

Harvey   If it landed here, then it's our responsibility.

Bart   Ah! And if we put it on another doorstep, then it's someone else's responsibility.

Harvey   Hello little fishy. Want to live with us?

Bart   Harvey, we have no idea how to take care of a goldfish.

Harvey   How hard can it be?

Bart   I know. A pet shelter.

Harvey   Hm?

Bart   That's the right thing to do. Bring it to a pet shelter.

Harvey   Oh. Of course.

Bart   Give it to me, I'll take it there now.

Harvey (*Doesn't move.*)   It's so cute, Bart.

Bart   Is it?

Harvey *makes a 'please' face.*

Bart   Okay. Give it to me.

Harvey   Let me take it.

Bart   I don't mind doing it.

Harvey   No, I want to. Leave it to me, Bart. This little fish and I are off to the pet shelter!

Scene 4

Song. At It Like Rabbits.

Rabbit   YOU'VE HEARD OF THE PHRASE
'AT IT LIKE RABBITS'
WELL IT'S NOT A PHRASE,
IT'S A FACT
AND I'M A DOE
WHO LIVES LIFE
LIKE THAT

ME AND MY MAN
AND WHAT A MAN
LOVED TO STAY UP AT NIGHT

WE'RE GREAT AT MAKING
BUNNIES
THE FIRST TIME ROUND
I PROUDLY COUNTED NINE

OUR OWNERS WEREN'T SO KEEN
WHEN THE NEXT BATCH
I POPPED OUT SEVENTEEN

THEY THOUGHT THERE'D BE NO
MORE
WE PROVED THEM WRONG
WITH A WHOPPER TWENTY-
FOUR

SO THAT WAS THE END
FOR ME AND MY MAN
AND WHAT A MAN
THEY SENT HIM OFF TO A FARM

Sound of a blade swishing.

AND I WAS SENT HERE
FOR SOME TIME TO MYSELF
A REFUGE FOR ME
AND ALL THE ANIMALS YOU SEE

IT'S JUST A PITSTOP
BEFORE I'M PICKED AND HEAD
OFF
TO MEET A NEW MAN
AND MAKE LOTS MORE BUNNIES!

All Pets   UNLOVED, REJECTED
SOME MALAISE DETECTED
BUT THAT'S OKAY
WE'RE SWADDLED IN HAY

UNLOVED, REJECTED
YOU'D NEVER QUITE SUSPECT IT
WE'RE FUN, WE'RE CUTE
WE'RE WAITING FOR YOU

COME HERE, COME GET US
WE'RE FLUFFY, WE'VE GOT
FEATHERS
STOP BY, AND CHOOSE US
AND WE'LL GO HOME
TOGETHER

HOORAY, HOORAY!
ANOTHER PLEASANT DAY
AT PET'ERNAL LOVE
WE'RE ON OUR WAY!
WE'LL BE OKAY!

Scene 5

Pet-Ernal Love Pet Shelter. The **Rabbit** *is in the pet shelter with a* **Cockatoo** *and a* **Mouse**. *The* **Pet Shelter Owner** (**PSO**) *enters. The phone rings.*

PSO   Hello, Pet'Ernal Love, it takes more work than you think. Mm. Terrapins are notorious for carrying salmonella. Mm. He shouldn't have handled it then. Mm. That's entirely the old man's fault. Mm. Terrapins aren't social pets, no. Mm. He died, did he? The old man. Mm. Bring him in. The Terrapin. And, if you need inspiration for the headstone, try – HE SHOULD NEVER HAVE TOUCHED HIS SHELL!

She hangs up.

           Song. Pet'Ernal Love.

PSO   PEOPLE REALLY ARE AN
                  ASTONISHING BREED
                  THEY TAKE WHAT THEY WANT
                  AND THEY DO AS THEY PLEASE

                  YOU'D THINK THAT WITH
                  THEIR OPPOSABLE THUMBS
                  THEY'D EVOLVED BEYOND
                  MEAN AND SELFISH POND SCUM

                  LOOK AT THIS MOUSE HERE
                  AS CUTE AS CAN BE
                  ABANDONED OUT THERE
                  IN A BOX ON THE STREET

                  HER OWNERS RAN OFF
                  LEFT A NOTE ON MY DOOR
                  YOURS IF YOU WANT, NOT OUR
                  PROBLEM ANYMORE!

                  HELLO, PET'ERNAL LOVE,
                  HOW DO YOU LIVE WITH

YOURSELF?
HELLO, PET'ERNAL LOVE,
ANOTHER PET FOR MY SHELF?
HELLO, PET'ERNAL LOVE,
YOU GOT A PET YOU REGRET?
HELLO?
WHY CAN'T YOU LOVE YOUR
PET ?!

Pets   BOOO HOOO HOOO

PEOPLE WILL HURT YOU
EVERYONE BUT ME
I'LL LOVE YOU FOREVER
HOLD TIGHT AND SQUEEZE
SHOW YOU I CARE
TIL YOU CAN'T BREATHE

Pets   YAY!

The phone rings.

Hello, Pet'Ernal Love, what if you're the mistake?

SO LIFE IS PRETTY TOUGH
FOR PEOPLE AS WELL
TURNS OUT THAT SHOWING
LOVE
CAN LAND A PERSON IN HELL

THERE WAS A LITTLE GIRL
WITH HOPE IN HER HEART
HER FATHER HAD A SHELTER
GIVING PETS A FRESH START

SHE BROUGHT AN
ADVERTISEMENT
INTO SCHOOL ONE DAY
ASKED IF ANY KIDS
COULD GIVE A HOME TO A
STRAY

THEY LAUGHED IN HER FACE
LEFT HER ALONE AND UPSET
THAT NIGHT HER FATHER SAID
'YOU ARE NEVER QUITE ALONE
WITH A PET'.

Pets   BOOOO HOOOO HOOOO

PEOPLE WILL HURT YOU
EVERYONE BUT ME
I'LL LOVE YOU FOREVER
HOLD TIGHT AND SQUEEZE
SHOW YOU I CARE
TIL YOU CAN'T BREATHE

Pet   YAY!

The phone rings.

Hello, Pet'Ernal Love, go on – break my heart!

SOME PEOPLE CRAVE
MATERNITY
SOME WANT TO BE PATERNAL
HAVE LOVE TO GIVE ETERNALLY
BUT ONLY FOR THEIR OWN
I'VE GROWN TO SEE THINGS
DIFFERENTLY
LOVE PETS UNCONDITIONALLY
AND SO
NONE OF THEM
NOT ONE OF THEM
WILL EVER FACE THE CRUELTY
OF PEOPLE AND THEIR TRUANCY
I'LL LOVE THEM ALL
PET'ERNALLY

I'll give them *all* a home!

The phone rings.

Hello, Pet'Ernal Love – just try a little harder!

The phone rings.

– Show me your ugly side!

The phone rings.

– Hit me with your hate stick!

The phone rings.

– We're open 'till five!

I AM AT CAPACITY,
FILLED MY AISLES AND SHELVES
THERE IS NO HUMANITY,
THEY THINK JUST OF
THEMSELVES.

THEY DING-A-LING UPON MY
DOOR,
MORE AND MORE EACH DAY
THEY CAN'T BEAR TO CARE
SO THEY THROW THEIR PETS
AWAY

I'D LOVE JUST ONCE IF WHEN
I WAS ANWERING THE PHONE
THE VOICE UPON
THE OTHER END
WAS OFFERING A HOME

OR CALLING AT THE DOOR
NOT TO DUMP BUT TO ASSIST
TO GIVE SUPPORT AND HOPE
AND HEY!
A REASON TO EXIST!

HELLO, PET'ERNAL LOVE,
HOW DO YOU LIVE WITH
YOURSELF?
HELLO, PET'ERNAL LOVE,
ANOTHER PET FOR MY SHELF?

HELLO, PET'ERNAL LOVE,
YOU GOT A PET YOU REGRET?
HELLO?
WHY CAN'T YOU LOVE YOUR
PET ?!

Ding-a-ling. **Harvey** *enters.*

Harvey   Hiya!

PSO   What do you want?

Harvey   It's not what I want, it's what I don't want actually.

Harvey *reveals the* **Goldfish**.

PSO   Win it in a raffle, did you?

Harvey   Hm?

PSO   First prize at the fair?

Harvey   No, it appeared on our doorstep. Turned up out of the blue.

PSO   Out of the blue, that's a new one. I've heard of lost and found, unwanted gifts, overcrowded ponds. But, out of the blue? Right, put it on the counter.

Harvey *places the* **Goldfish** *on the counter. The* **PSO** *starts to unpack her 'fish-checking apparatus', goggles, gloves, headlamp, etc.*

PSO   People like you make me sick. No consideration for vulnerable little things.

Harvey   That's not true.

PSO (*mimicking him*)   'It's not what I want, it's what I don't want actually.'

Harvey   I didn't mean it like that.

PSO   You don't care about this little fish. You're disgusting.

Harvey   Hey!

PSO (*examining the fish*)   Right, let's have a look at this little swimmer. It's not an Aranda, that's for sure. And there aren't any tell-tale signs that indicate Shebunkin, Catacult or Coy.

Harvey   I think it's a little coy actually.

PSO   It's not a Comet, nor a Serassa. Maybe a cousin of the Pearl Scale, or a descendent of the Red Cap, but no. No tell-tale signs. Where did you say it came from again?

Harvey   Out of the blue.

PSO   You're sticking to that line I see. Well, I can safely say whatever species of fish this is, it's certainly not one I've ever seen before. (*She takes out a form, and writes.*) Species unknown. Not to worry little fish, you're safe here with me. (*To* **Harvey**) Sign here, and then get out.

Harvey *grabs the fish off the counter.*

PSO   What are you doing?

Harvey   I've changed my mind.

PSO   What?

Harvey   The fish comes home with me.

PSO   Oh, you have a heart now, do you?

Harvey   I've always had a heart.

PSO   You don't seem like a very stable person to me.

Harvey   I'm as stable as I can be, all things considered.

PSO   How do I know this fish is going to be safe with you?

Harvey   Because I said so.

PSO   Wow, compelling. Little man – I've seen the terrible things humans are capable of. It's a man eat dog world out there.

Harvey   I don't eat dogs.

PSO   It seems I'm faced with two options here. Option one, wrestle you to the floor and extract that fish from your ferocious grip . . . or, two . . . take your word and trust you. I'm inclined to go for option one, but I've got a bad wrist and a dodgy left knee, which means my wrestling days are behind me. So, listen up.

> GIVE IT FISH FOOD
> TWICE A DAY
> A PINCH OR TWO
> SHOULD BE OKAY
> AND CYCLED WATER
> FOR THE TANK
> NOW DON'T USE TAP
> IT GETS TOO RANK
> PEBBLES FOR THE FLOOR,
> WITH WEEDS
> AND SPARSE WITH DECORATION
> PLEASE
> AND DON'T FORGET TO
> KEEP IT CLEAN
> AND OXYGEN FOR BREATHING
> IN

Harvey
> I WISH YOU WOULD SLOW
> DOWN
> I HAVE NO IDEA WHAT YOU'RE
> SAYING

Breathing. Okay.

PSO
> KEEP THE WATER
> BALANCED AND THEN
> TEST THE HEATING

WITH YOUR HAND
TO STOP THE FISH
GETTING THE HUMP
YOU START IT OFF
WITH THIS NEW PUMP

Harvey   THIS IS SO CONFUSING
SO MANY WORDS
BUT I LIKE USING PICTURES

Did you say pump?

PSO   TAKE THESE PEBBLES
FOR THE FLOOR
THIS PUMP I MENTIONED
ONCE BEFORE
AND CYCLED WATER
THAT'S GERM FREE
ONE NET, NO TWO, OKAY TAKE
THREE

Harvey   IT'S ACTUALLY QUITE
IMPRESSIVE
YOU SEEM TO SPEAK
WITHOUT
NEEDING TO BREATHE AT ALL

PSO   ONCE YOU HAVE ALL THIS SET
UP
TRANSFER THE FISH INTO ITS
HOME
THE SPACE IS SMALL AND NEEDS
SOME LIFE
TRY THIS SPACE MAN AND HIS
SPACE WIFE FOR
DECORATION

Harvey   OKAY NOW I'M PANICKING

THIS WALL OF NOISE HAS
REALLY GOT ME –

Decoration? Oh, that won't be a problem. I'll gussy up that bowl.

PSO   Bowl?

Harvey   Yes, the goldfish bowl.

PSO   No bowl.

Harvey   No bowl?

PSO   Yes, no bowl.

Harvey   Snow bowl?

PSO   No! No bowl.

Harvey   No bowl.

PSO   Yes.

Harvey   Yes?

PSO   No.

Harvey   No?

PSO   Bowl.

Harvey   Nono Bowl?

PSO   Somebody help me.

Cockatoo   Help me.

PSO   LITTLE MAN
                PROVE YOURSELF
                GIVE SOME HOPE TO ME

DO RIGHT BY
THIS LITTLE FISH
MAKE UP FOR ALL HUMANITY

DON'T YOU SCREW IT UP,
DON'T YOU MAKE MISTAKES
DON'T YOU, DON'T YOU FAIL.

Act 2

Scene 1

Harvey *is alone with the fish.*

Song. Fishy Feelings.

Harvey   EM, OKAY.
THAT DIDN'T GO GREAT.

RIGHT, LET'S SEE –
I'VE STILL GOT THE FISH?

HUH, THAT'S STRANGE
THAT SPARKLE INSIDE

SO I GUESS
YOU'RE COMING WITH ME

NOT REALLY SURE WHAT
HAPPENED
OR WHAT THAT LADY SAID
I'M NOT THAT GOOD AT
LISTENING
THINGS FLY OUT OF MY LITTLE
HEAD

OH YOU
ARE CUTE
WHAT'S HAP'NING TO ME?

All   FISH-Y
FISHY WISHY
FISHY
FISHY WISHY

Harvey *is back home with all of the goldfish paraphernalia.*
Bart *sees him.*

Bart   What's that?

Harvey   An air purifier. No, wait, an oxygen pump. I think.

Bart   And that?

Harvey   Food. Or else some kind of chemical for the pump. Definitely one or the other.

Bart   That's helpful. And that?

Harvey   Not sure what that is.

Harvey *reveals the fish from behind his back.*

Bart	HEY, HARVEY WHAT'S THAT IN THE BAG?
Harvey	SO, SURPRISE! I BROUGHT HOME THE FISH!
Bart	BUT, I THOUGHT WE AGREED IT WOULD GO?
Harvey	YEAH, AND NO I COULDN'T LET GO BART, I AM FEELING SOMETHING I COULDN'T GIVE THE FISH AWAY I DON'T KNOW WHAT'S HAPPENING

Bart   That's fine, I'll take care of it.

Bart *grabs the bag from* **Harvey**, *and in the process punctures a small hole in it. Water begins to spray out'.*

Harvey	WOAH THE BAG IT'S SPRUNG A LEAK
Bart	JUST STAY CALM THERE'S NO NEED TO FREAK GRAB THE TANK WATCH OUT FOR THAT YOKE

In the panic, **Harvey** *drops the tank and it smashes.*

Harvey	OH NOT GOOD THE TANK HAS JUST BROKE
Bart	THE BOWL THE BOWL WE'LL USE THE CRYSTAL BOWL
Harvey	NO BOWL!
Bart	NO BOWL?
Harvey	THE LADY SAID NO BOWL!
Bart	NO BOWL?
Harvey	NO BOWL.
Bart	WHY NOT?
Harvey	NO BOWL.
Bart	HARVEY – USE WORDS!
Harvey	NO NO NO NO NO BOWL.
Bart	I NEVER SHOULD HAVE TRUSTED YOU TO RID US OF THIS FISH ISSUE THE ONLY WAY TO DO THINGS IS TO DO THEM BY YOURSELF

Bart   Okay, water.

Harvey   Don't use tap water!

Bart   What?

Harvey   Tap water. Bad.

Bart   Then what kind of water?!?

Harvey   Em . . . Oh?

Bart   Come on, Harvey.

Harvey   I can't remember what she said.

Bart   Mineral water?

Harvey   She spoke so fast.

Bart   Sparkling?

Harvey   There's only a mouthful of water left in the bag.

Bart   I'm using tap water.

Harvey   The fish is going to die!

Bart (*as he fills the bowl with tap water*)   A mouthful? Who measures things in mouthfuls?

Harvey *looks at the fish in the bag and swigs the fish into his mouth.*

Bart   Okay, water is in the bowl.

Harvey   MMM.

Bart   Give me the fish.

Harvey   MMM.

Bart   Harvey?

Harvey   MMM.

Bart   Hello?

Harvey   MMM.

Bart   Where is the fish?

Harvey *grabs* **Bart** *and plants a kiss on his mouth. In that moment the fish passes from* **Harvey**'s *mouth into* **Bart**'s *mouth.*

Harvey   The fish is in your mouth!

All   OOOH.

Bart   MMM!

Harvey	I FEEL QUITE STRANGE
Bart	MMM.
Harvey	LIKE SOMETHING'S ABOUT TO CHANGE
Bart	MMM.
Harvey	WHAT IF IT'S THE START OF SOMETHING NEW NEW FOR ME AND YOU?

Bart *rushes past* **Harvey** *and spits the fish into the bowl.*

Bart   Ugh. Harvey, don't ever do that again.

Harvey   Bart, look.

They look at the fish.

Bart   Harvey. We can't do this.

Harvey   But Bart, we *are* doing it. This is us doing it right now. Look at fishy, so happy. Swimming about in its new little house. Here with us.

Bart   The fish was just in my mouth, Harvey. It almost died. You need to bring all of this stuff back to the pet shelter.

Harvey   I can't. The tank is cracked. And the lady, she's . . . kind of scary.

Bart   I should have just taken it there myself.

Harvey   But Bart?

Bart   I'll bring the tank to Tom and Sandra's. She'll fix it, she's practical like that. Then when I come back, we are returning everything, including the fish.

Harvey   Bart.

Bart   No.

Scene 2

Sandra *and* **Tom***'s home.* **Sandra** *is holding Josie and Jimmy.* **Tom** *has Patsy in his arms and Greggles is lying down on a changing mat.* **Tom** *and* **Sandra** *want their babies to sleep.*

Sandra   Did you pack the paddling pool?

Tom   Paddling pool.

Sandra   Is that a no?

Tom   It's a maybe, I actually can't remember. I'm delirious, Sandra. I sometimes struggle to remember what age I am.

Sandra   Tom, please. Check the list, cross things off. I don't want to forget anything.

Tom   Like telling your best friend that we're moving?

Sandra   I am going to tell him.

Tom   When?

Sandra   Oh please Tom, you don't understand.

Tom   Understand what?

Sandra   Bart. He's very . . . funny about things like this. He won't take it well.

Tom   You're right, I don't understand.

Sandra   Bart and I were like brother and sister growing up, we still are. I know him, I need to tell him calmly and carefully.

Tom   Greggles has that cranky look in his eye. He needs to nap.

Sandra   I know, Josie, Jimmy and Patsy do too.

Song. Sleep Baby Sleep.

Tom   SLEEP, BABY SLEEP
                            GO TO SLEEP WE BEG YOU
                            SLEEP, BABY SLEEP

Sandra	I'M SO FRICKIN TIRED
Tom	GIVE US TIME
Sandra	I LOVE YOU MY BABIES
Tom	WE SHOULD FINISH PACKING THAT LAMP NEEDS WRAPPING AND THE KITCHEN FLOORS COULD DO WITH A SWEEP
Sandra	WE'LL GET BACK TO PACKING WHILE THEY ARE NAPPING THOUGH I'D REALLY LIKE TO HAVE A SLEEP MYSELF
Both	HA HA HA HA HA HA HA HA WE HAVE FOUR BABIES NEVER EVER SLEEP NEVER EVER EVER SO WE LIFT AND WE FEED WE'RE WASHING BABYGROWS AT HIGH SPEED FINDING GREAT DEALS ON BABY FOOD MEALS AND ON NAPPIES AND ON DODIES AND ON BOOTIES FOR THEIR TOESIES CLEANING BOTTLE WARMING KITS CHECKING THE BASSINETS ARE CLEAN
Tom	AND HAVE A MOISTURISING REIGIME!
Both	AND EXERCISE AND NOT TO FIGHT IN THE HOUR WE HAVE AT NIGHT

AND HOLDING DOWN FULL-TIME
JOBS
TO COVER THE COST OF BITS
AND BOBS
THERE'S ALWAYS ONE MORE
THING
THERE'S ALWAYS ONE MORE
THING
THERE'S ALWAYS ONE MORE
THING
ARE THEY AWAKE?
OH

Tom   SLEEP, BABY SLEEP
GO TO SLEEP WE BEG YOU
SLEEP BABY SLEEP

Sandra   THEY'RE FALLING ASLEEP

Both   WE'RE SO TIRED
THEY'RE ALL ASLEEP NOW

Silence and calm. Then, the sound of an elaborate doorbell.
Tom *and* **Sandra** *freeze.*

Tom (*whispering*)   No.

Sandra (*trying to send the message telepathically*)   Stay asleep.

Tom   I will donate a kidney right now if you all stay asleep.

Bart *enters with the tank.*

Bart   Hey guys! I knew you were home. No one answered the door, so I let myself in with my key.

Tom (*whispering*)   Hey Brian, the babies are asleep.

Bart   My name is Bart.

Tom   Sorry.

Bart   You keep doing that.

Tom   Baby brain. There's a lot of names flying about.

Sandra (*whispering*)   Bart, the babies are asleep.

Tom   All four of them, at the same time.

Sandra   It's like a miracle.

Tom   Like winning the lotto and cashing the cheque and flying away from where you live to a private island where no one knows you. Then buying a boat and sailing out into the middle of the ocean. Then standing completely naked on the helm and roaring mindlessly into the sunset to remind yourself that you do in fact exist.

Sandra   So, em, we'll keep it down – if that's alright.

Bart   Yeah, of course.

Sandra   What's the tank for?

Bart   A goldfish. It landed on our doorstep completely out of the blue. So Harvey went to give it to a pet shelter, but I think he got a bit confused. Anyway, long story. I need to repair this crack in the tank or else we can't return it. Do you guys have any glass glue?

Bart *turns to place the tank where a side table used to be. It slams to the floor with a bang. They all gasp.*

Bart   Sorry. I thought there was a table there.

Baby 1   WAAAAAAAA
                    WAAAAAAAA
                    WAAAAAAAA

Sandra   Ah crap.

Tom   There was a table there.

Sandra   It's gone now.

Bart   Where is all your stuff? Are you guys renovating?

Tom   I'll sort this, don't want it to spread.

Sandra   The crying is infectious.

Tom   Time for you and Bart to have *that* chat.

Tom *goes to the crying baby.*

Bart   What chat?

Baby 2   WAAAAAAAA
                          WAAAAAAAA
                          WAAAAAAAA

Tom   That's the second one kicking off. It's spreading.

Bart   WASN'T THERE A
                          TELLY OVER THERE?
                          WHERE WE'D WATCH TV
                          AND EAT OUR BODY WEIGHT IN
                          CHEESE?

Sandra   Yep.

Bart   WHERE'S THE VELVET COUCH
                          AND YOUR WEIRD LAMP?
                          WHERE'S TOM'S MINIBAR?

Sandra   THEY'RE NOT
                          THERE ANYMORE.

Tom *has come back, and hands Patsy to* **Bart** *and Greggles to*
Sandra.

Tom   TELL HIM.

Bart   Sandra, what is going on?

                          HIYA JOSIE.

Tom   THAT'S PATSY
                          TELL HIM SANDRA

Baby 3   WAAAAAAAA
                          WAAAAAAAA
                          WAAAAAAAA

Tom *leaves to get Josie.*

Sandra   YOU KNOW HOW BADLY
                          I WANTED A BABY

Bart	WE TALKED ABOUT IT ENDLESSLY
Sandra	IT WAS EVERYTHING I EVER WANTED EVER EVER AND WE STRUGGLED WE NEEDED HELP COULDN'T MAKE IT HAPPEN YOU CAN'T GET THEM OFF THE SHELF WE JUST WANTED ONE, TO START AND MORE IF WE WERE LUCKY WE WENT TO THE DOCTOR LOADS AND LOADS AND LOADS TRIED AND TRIED AND TOLD HER TO LASH IN THEM EMBRYOS
Bart	AND SHE DID
Sandra & Tom	AND INSTEAD OF ONE WE HAD FOUR!
Baby 4	WAAAAAAAA WAAAAAAAA WAAAAAAAA

Tom *has to go get Jimmy.*

Babies	WAAAAAAAA WAAAAAAAA WAAAAAAAA

Tom *is back holding Josie and Jimmy.*

Sandra	AND FOUR IS FOUR TIMES MORE THAN ONE
Tom	IT IS TWO TIMES MORE THAN TWO

Both	WE HADN'T PREPARED FOR THIS AT ALL WE HAVE BITTEN OFF MORE THAN WE CAN CHEW
Babies	WAAAAAAAA WAAAAAAAA WAAAAAAAA
Tom	SANDRA TELL HIM.
Bart	TELL ME WHAT?
Sandra	THAT WE'RE LEAVING

Bart   What? When?

Sandra	SOON, VERY SOON WE NEED MORE PEOPLE TO HELP US
Tom	WE HAVE TO GO WE'RE MOVING HOME
Bart	HOME? WHERE?
Tom	TO WHERE I'M FROM NEAR MY FAMILY WE NEED MORE HELP
Sandra & Tom	WE HAVE QUADRUPLETS!

Bart   I can help with the babies.

Sandra   I know, I know you can but –

Tom   We need a different kind of help.

Sandra   We need family.

Bart	I THOUGHT THAT WE WERE FAMILY
Sandra	OH WE ARE FAMILY BART, THAT WILL NEVER CHANGE

Tom	NEVER EVER
Bart	WHEN ARE YOU LEAVING?
Sandra	TOMORROW.
Bart	OH TOMORROW?
Tom	YES.
Bart	THAT'S SOON
Sandra	VERY SOON
Tom	IN THE MORNING, YES. IT'S SOON
Bart	VERY SOON.
Babies	WAAAAAAAA WAAAAAAAA WAAAAAAAA
Bart	OKAY.

Sandra   Do you still want the glass glue? I can try and root it out.

Bart	NO, IT'S FINE.

I'm gonna go. (*About Greggles*) Can I give you . . .

Tom   Greggles. It's grand, they all look the same.

Bart *hands Greggles back to* **Tom***, then picks up the cracked tank.*

Sandra   I'll still see you all the time. Nothing is going to change. We just needed a bit more space, and help, that's all.

Bart   Of course, yeah.

Sandra   Love you pal.

Bart   You too.

Tom   Bart!

Bart   What?

Tom   Nothing, I just wanted to prove I know your name.

Bart *leaves with the tank under his arm.*

Tom	SLEEP, BABY SLEEP GO TO SLEEP WE BEG YOU SLEEP, BABY SLEEP
Sandra	I THINK HE'S UPSET
Tom	HE'LL BE FINE CAN WE GO TO SLEEP NOW?
Tom, Sandra & Babies	WAAAAAAAAAAA!

Scene 3

Deirdre *is at* **Harvey***'s front door, dressed as a weather system.*

Deirdre   What am I?

Harvey   Ooh. A hairy lemon?

Deirdre   No. I knew it was crap. I'm a weather system.

Harvey   Oh?

Deirdre   That bit is a cloud. If you squeeze it, it rains. See.

Harvey   I see it now.

Deirdre   I've had to improvise with this one. Last-minute booking for a child's birthday who doesn't want to go outside. So his family wanted to bring the outside in. Ta da! Anyway, do you have twenty quid? I couldn't fit into the bus, so I need to book a people carrier.

Harvey   Yeah, let me check my purse.

Deirdre (*about the fish*)   What's that?

Harvey   A goldfish.

Deirdre   I didn't know you guys got a goldfish.

Harvey   We didn't. It landed on our doorstep.

Deirdre   On its own?

Harvey   Yeah.

Deirdre   I've heard about things like that.

Harvey   Bart doesn't want it to stay. He thinks we're not able for it.

Deirdre   He's not great with curve balls.

Harvey   No. So he's gone to Sandra and Tom's house to fix the tank. Then he said we're bringing everything back to the pet shelter. Including the fish.

Deirdre   And how do you feel about that?

Harvey *makes a sad face.*

Deirdre   Your face makes me think that you're sad about that.

Harvey   Well, it kind of makes me question whether . . .

Deirdre   Yeah.

Harvey   If Bart wants one thing and I want something else . . .

Deirdre   You're not finishing your sentences there, pal.

Harvey   I kind of wonder if . . . I don't want to say.

Deirdre   Sometimes when I have something difficult that I want to say, or hard questions that I need to ask I pretend that I'm asking for a friend.

Harvey   What do you mean?

Song. Asking for a Friend.

Deirdre   IF YOU HAVE
                         SOMETHING TO ASK
                         BUT YOU'RE AFRAID
                         OR IT'S TOO HARD
                         TO ASK IT
                         JUST PRETEND
                         YOU'RE ASKING FOR A FRIEND

Harvey   Do you mean lying?

Deirdre   No, it's not lying at all. It's more like hiding.

Harvey   How does it work then?

Deirdre   Okay, so . . .

                         I'VE GOT A FRIEND
                         WORKS WITH KIDS

GLUED HER FOOT
TO THE CHEEK OF A BOY
THEY ARE GONNA SUE
SHOULD SHE CHANGE HER
NAME?

Harvey   I'm confused. Deirdre, are you being sued?

Deirdre

NO, NO I'M NOT
BECAUSE THERE IS NO FRIEND
THE FRIEND ISN'T REAL
I JUST PRETEND
TO ASK FOR A FRIEND

Harvey   Oh!

Deirdre   See, it's fun. You try!

Harvey   Em, okay.

I'VE GOT A FRIEND
FOUND A FISH
HE WANTS IT
BUT HIS HUSBAND WANTS IT
GONE
WHAT SHOULD HE DO?
JUST ASKING FOR A FRIEND.

Deirdre   Who does he want more, his husband or the fish?

Harvey   You can't ask me that!

Deirdre   Only messing. Go on!

Harvey

I'VE GOT A FRIEND
WHO HAS A FEELING
THAT HIS FISH
IS THE START OF SOMETHING
NEW
BUT THE END OF SOMETHING
TOO
AND MY FRIEND IS KIND OF
SCARED

Deirdre   What's your friend scared of?

Harvey   Not following his gut. Hurting Bart . . . I mean, his husband. My friend, my friend's husband . . . Burt. Anyway

> THERE IS NO FRIEND
> MY FRIEND ISN'T REAL
> I JUST PRETEND
> TO ASK FOR A FRIEND

Deirdre   Now you've got it. Go again! Really lean in this time.

Harvey

> I'VE GOT A FRIEND
> WHO DIDN'T LISTEN
> WHEN HE WAS TOLD
> HOW TO CARE FOR THE FISH
> IS THIS A MISTAKE?
> IS HE GOOD ENOUGH?

Deirdre   Good enough? Why?

Harvey

> COZ HE DOESN'T KNOW
> WHAT HE'S DOING.
> IN OVER HIS HEAD
> AND OUT OF HIS DEPTH
> JUST ASKING FOR A FRIEND

Deirdre   Hmm, doesn't seem to be any obvious solutions.

Harvey   If that scary pet shelter owner lady knew I had no idea what I was doing she'd take the fish away. Maybe that would be the best thing, maybe then my problems would be solved. And things would go back to the way they were before . . . for my friend.

Deirdre   Oh! Interesting.

> RIGHT MY FRIEND
> SOUNDS LIKE YOUR TROUBLED
> FRIEND

IS AT AN AWKWARD BEND
AND I WOULD RECOMMEND
THAT HE ASK A FRIEND
ON WHOM HE CAN DEPEND
TO INTERVENE
AND SOLVE HIS PRESENT WOES

Harvey   That would be great! I'd love that.

Deirdre

LEAVE IT TO ME
OR SHOULD I SAY TO MY FRIEND
YOU DON'T HAVE TO WORRY
IT'LL WORK OUT IN THE END

Harvey   Yay!

Both

THERE ARE NO PROBLEMS WHEN YOU'RE
ASKING FOR A FRIEND
YOUR PROBLEMS DON'T EXIST
THEY BELONG TO YOUR FRIEND

IF YOU'RE AFRAID
JUST ASK FOR A FRIEND
A THING YOU CAN'T SAY
JUST ASK FOR A FRIEND.
THROW CLARITY AWAY
DON'T BE DIRECT AGAIN
JUST ASK FOR
ASK FOR A FRIEND

Deirdre   I'm still going to need that twenty quid.

Harvey   Oh yeah, here.

Deirdre   I'll sort this for you, pal.

Harvey   What are you going to do?

Deirdre   Exactly what your friend needs me to do.

Harvey *leaves*.

Deirdre   EVERYTHING'S OKAY
                          YOU'VE ASKED FOR A FRIEND
                          THROW WORRY AWAY
                          YOU'VE ASKED FOR A FRIEND
                          I'LL SAVE THE DAY
                          AND BRING THIS TO AN END
                          I'LL FIX THIS
                          FOR YOU
                          MY FRIEND!

Scene 4

Pet'Ernal Love Pet Shelter. The **Terrapin** *is now among the pets in the shelter.*

PSO   What do you want?

Deirdre   That's a very confrontational way to greet a potential customer.

PSO   Are you a potential customer?

Deirdre   Maybe.

PSO   Please get out.

Deirdre   Having a bad day?

PSO   Are there good days?

Deirdre   Dark.

PSO   I can go darker, try me.

Deirdre   What is it, man trouble? Woman trouble?

PSO   Yes, both of those things and all of the above multiplied by 7.9 billion. People trouble. People are trouble. You're people, and I'm troubled. So, get out.

Cockatoo   Get out.

Deirdre   Well, look at you. Aren't you pretty?

Cockatoo   Aren't you pretty?

Deirdre   Me? Thank you. Hey! Would you like to come home with me?

PSO   Absolutely not.

Deirdre   Oh. I see. You drive a hard bargain. (*taking out the money* **Harvey** *gave her*) How about I sweeten things with this crisp twenty?

Cockatoo   Crisp twenty.

PSO   Let me be perfectly clear with you, sunshine.

Deirdre   Weather system.

PSO   Whatever. These animals have been through the mill. Rejected, cast out, spurned by people like you. It takes a very special kind of person to give them the love that they need.

Deirdre   I'm a special person.

PSO   Yes you are.

Deirdre   Thanks.

PSO   There is no way that I'm allowing a woman dressed as a life boat –

Deirdre   Weather system.

PSO   – to take one of my precious pets away from me. From here, I mean. So the answer is no.

Deirdre   You don't have a lot of hope in humanity.

PSO   Bingo. People are not my people. Pets are my people. So, goodbye.

Deirdre   It's sad to think of people hurting them.

PSO   What?

Deirdre   People. Hurting pets. On purpose.

PSO   People hurting pets on purpose?

Deirdre   Lady, I know people who are being cruel to a pet.

PSO   Don't play tricks with me.

Deirdre   This is no trick. There are two of them.

PSO   And the pet?

Deirdre   A helpless little goldfish.

PSO   A goldfish?

Deirdre   Yes! And these two evil torturers, the things they're getting up to. They are flinging it around the place.

Cockatoo   Flinging it around the place.

Deirdre   And crisping its skin with a blowtorch.

Cockatoo   With a blowtorch.

Deirdre   And tattooing eyes on its tail so it looks back to front.

Cockatoo   Back to front.

Deirdre   And planning to turn it into sushi.

Cockatoo   Sushi.

PSO   I'm going to be sick. I'm ashamed to call myself a human.

Deirdre   The fish needs a hero.

Cockatoo   A hero.

Deirdre   And that hero, in the right outfit, could be you.

PSO   Where are they?

Deirdre   I have the address right here, conveniently written out on a piece of paper.

PSO   Right, this is a rescue mission.

The **PSO** *pulls out a 'fish rescue kit' that includes a scooper of some kind to retrieve it.*

Deirdre   Did I mention that they were blowtorching the fish's skin?

Cockatoo   Yes you did!

PSO   Give me that address!

Deirdre   You really think there is something you can do?

PSO   There is no one better equipped than me.

Deirdre   Oh, how wonderful. I just couldn't sleep knowing the heinous crimes against goldfish that these two monsters are committing.

PSO   Get out of my way.

Deirdre (*offering the twenty*)   Here, take a cab.

PSO   Oh, thanks!

Deirdre   Get there faster.

PSO   No time to waste.

Deirdre   Go. Quick. Fly.

The **PSO** *runs out of the shop.*

Deirdre   That one's for you, Harvey, you're welcome!

Deirdre *leaves. The* **Terrapin** *trots forward.*

Song. Terrapin Plea.

Terrapin

I AM A TERRAPIN
DON'T TOUCH ME, FELLA
IT'S VERY POSSIBLE
I'VE GOT SALMONELLA

MY LAST OWNER DIED
HE TOUCHED MY SHELL
NOT A NICE GUY
SO HE CAN BURN IN HELL

I HAVE A TEMPER
CAN SOMETIMES ATTACK
OTHER THAN ALL OF THAT
I'M FANTASTIC CRAIC

PICK ME, PICK ME
PICK ME, PICK ME

Scene 5

Bart *is stood staring at the* **Goldfish**. **Harvey** *enters.*

Harvey   Oh, Bart. You're home. Where's the fish tank?

Bart   Pack up the fish.

Harvey   Wait, I know what I've been feeling now –

Bart   Pack up the fish and let's go.

Harvey   I don't want to. I can't.

Bart   Why not?

Harvey   Because I love the fish.

Bart   What?

Harvey   I love the fish. With all of my heart.

Bart   Love it? What are you talking about? It landed at our door a few hours ago, how can you love it?

Harvey   It's everything I've ever wanted.

Bart   Harvey? I thought I was –

Harvey   This is what is next for us, Bart.

Bart   This random goldfish?

Harvey   It's not just a random goldfish. Now I don't know where it came from, because I'm not a cosmologist. What I do know for sure is that Fishy needs us.

Bart   Fishy?

Harvey   Yeah, Fishy. That's what I'm calling it, for now.

Bart   And you love it?

Harvey   Dearly.

Harvey *goes to the fish, he's happy.* **Bart** *sees this, joins him.*

Bart   Do you think it's hungry?

Harvey   Maybe.

Bart   Okay. Which of these did you say was the food?

Harvey   The one that says food.

Bart   None of them say food.

Harvey   Em, that one. (*Under his breath*) I think.

Bart *sprinkles something into the bowl.*

Harvey   Does this mean you've changed your mind about the fish?

Bart   If you love it, Harvey?

Harvey   I do.

Bart   Then, yes.

Harvey   Yay! Let's think about a name?

Bart   Seems low on the list of priorities, but okay.

Harvey   I like the sound of Brenda.

Bart   Brenda?

Harvey   Yeah, Brenda the goldfish.

Bart   Em, I'm not sure.

Harvey   Okay, if not Brenda then Glen?

Bart   Harvey, I'm a bit scared. You know what you're doing here, right? You know how to take care of Fishy?

Harvey   Yes, I do.

Bart   Promise.

Harvey   Pinky promise.

They kiss. Doorbell. The **PSO** *arrives, with her fish rescue kit and an attitude.*

Song. Careless People.

PSO GOOD EVENING SIR
WE'VE NOT MET BEFORE
I WON'T WASTE
MUCH OF YOUR TIME.
YOU'VE GOT A GOLDFISH
THAT I'VE COME FOR
IT'S TIME TO SAY
YOUR GOODBYES.

Bart GOOD EVENING MADAM,
HOW KIND OF YOU TO CALL
I'VE NOT HEARD MUCH
ABOUT YOU EITHER
YOU NEEDN'T WORRY
YOURSELF AT ALL
WE'VE DECIDED
THAT WE'RE GOING TO KEEP IT.

PSO MY SOURCES TELL ME
QUITE RELIABLY
YOU'RE BEING CRUEL
TO AN INNOCENT FISH

Bart YOU ARE MISTAKEN
THERE IS NO CRUELTY HERE
TAKE A LOOK
IF YOU WISH

Harvey Hiya!

PSO You.

Harvey Me.

The **PSO** *sees the punch bowl.*

PSO Is that fish in a bowl?

Harvey Oh bowl?

PSO   No bowl.

Harvey   No bowl. You did say not to do that.

Bart   That's a crystal punch bowl in fact, holds twenty cups.

PSO   Where's the tank?

Bart   Oh the tank smashed, beyond repair.

PSO   Where is the oxygen pump?

Bart   The what?

PSO   No decoration, no plants, no weeds.

Bart   Decoration? Do you mean the pebbles?

Harvey   We just em . . . hadn't gotten round to that yet.

Bart   We were actually just feeding it.

Bart *holds up the feed. The* **PSO** *snatches it from him.*

PSO   This isn't food. It's chemical tank cleaner.

Bart   Tank cleaner? Harvey?

Harvey   My mistake.

Bart   Your mistake?

PSO   Your mistake! Is the water cycled?

Harvey   To be honest I don't know what that is.

PSO   Cycled water! I told you.

Harvey   Did you?

Bart   It's tap water.

PSO   TAP!

WHAT'S GOING ON HERE
I THOUGHT I WAS CLEAR
WHEN I TOLD YOU WHAT TO DO

Harvey   I KNOW I HAVEN'T
BEEN PERFECT
IN MY ATTEMPT
TO PROTECT
THIS GOLD
SWIMMING IN THE BLUE
HAVING HAD TIME TO REFLECT
I'M VERY CLEAR ABOUT
NEGLECT
AND NOW KNOW WHAT TO DO

PSO   ENOUGH WITH YOUR EXCUSES
THE TWO OF YOU ARE USELESS
THIS FISH IS IN FEAR
FOR ITS LIFE

Bart   HARVEY YOU LIED
TO ME JUST NOW
WHEN YOU SAID
THAT YOU KNEW HOW
TO TAKE CARE OF
THIS LITTLE FISH

PSO   THIS GRUESOME
DANGEROUS NASTY PLACE
IS NO SAFE HARBOUR
IT'S UNSAFE
AS FOR YOU TWO
SELFISH MEN
YOU'LL NEVER SEE THIS
FISH AGAIN

Bart   DON'T SPEAK TO
US LIKE THAT
YOU DON'T KNOW US
AT ALL

PSO   I PLACED HOPE IN YOU
TRUSTED YOU'D COME
THROUGH

	BUT YOU'RE MONSTERS LIKE ALL HUMANITY!
Bart & Harvey	STOP!
PSO	YOU'RE CARELESS PEOPLE
Bart & Harvey	NO!
PSO	BAD PEOPLE
All	WHAT?
PSO	YOU'RE NOT SUITABLE
All	NO
PSO	NOT GOOD ENOUGH
All	NO
PSO	TO TAKE CARE OF ANOTHER LIVING THING!

The **PSO** *scoops the fish into a bag.*

Harvey	DON'T TAKE THE FISH AWAY FROM ME I LOVE THE FISH SO DEARLY PLEASE, WE'RE A FAMILY

PSO   Family, ha! You're not even the same species.

Harvey	NO DON'T TAKE FISHY FISHY WISHY PLEASE BART DO SOMETHING PLEASE STOP HER TAKING FISHY BART DO SOMETHING BART DO SOMETHING

The **PSO** *is gone.*

Bart   You said you knew what you were doing.

Harvey   There were so many instructions, Bart. She speaks so fast.

Bart   What did you think was going to happen? The fish had no oxygen, we were feeding it chemicals.

Harvey   I didn't know they were chemicals.

Bart   This is all your fault.

Harvey   What?

Bart   YOU SHOULD NOT
                    HAVE BROUGHT IT HOME
                    YOU SHOULDA LEFT
                    THE FISH ALONE
                    YOU ARE OUT
                    OF YOUR DEPTH
                    YOU HAVE REALLY
                    OVERSTEPPED
                    YOU PUT THE FISH
                    INTO A BOWL
                    YOU WERE CLEARLY
                    TOLD NOT TO
                    YOU PROMISED ME
                    YOU DIDN'T LISTEN
                    CAREFULLY
                    NOW LOOK
                    WHAT YOU'VE DONE
                    SHE'S RIGHT
                    YOU'RE NOT ABLE
                    TO CARE
                    FOR ANOTHER
                    LIVING THING

Harvey   Bart, how can you say that to me?

Bart   Look, just forget it. It's fine. The fish is gone, it's over now. I forgive you.

Harvey   Oh. Bart.

Harvey *decides to leave.*

Bart   Where are you going?

Harvey   I'm going to have a sleepover at Deirdre's house.

Bart   Why? I said everything was fine.

Harvey *doesn't say anything.*

Bart   WILL YOU BE BACK
                          IN THE MORNING?

Harvey *leaves.*

                          OKAY, I'LL SEE YOU
                          IN THE MORNING THEN.
                          HE'S COMING BACK IN THE
                          MORNING
                          EVERYTHING IS FORGIVEN.
                          OH.
                          WHAT A CRAZY DAY
                          WHAT A CRAZY DAY.
                          AND NOW THE FISH IS GONE.
                          NO, BETTER OFF NOW IT'S GONE.
                          AND
                          HARVEY WILL COME BACK
                          HE'LL COME BACK IN THE
                          MORNING.
                          I'M EVERYTHING HE WANTS
                          YES, HE'LL BE BACK IN THE
                          MORNING
                          NO
                          SANDRA'S MOVING OUT
                          SHE'S LEAVING IN THE
                          MORNING.
                          I DON'T NEED HER ANYWAY.
                          EVERYTHING IS FINE.
                          NO,
                          EVERYTHING IS FINE.
                          I'M ACTUALLY DELIGHTED

A LITTLE PEACE AND QUIET.
I GOT JUST WHAT I WANTED
THEY'LL ALL BE BACK IN THE
MORNING.
OH NOW I CAN'T WAIT FOR THE
MORNING.
ROLL ON TOMORROW
MORNING!
FABULOUS NEW
MORNING.
NO, HE'LL BE BACK IN THE
MORNING.
I WON'T BE ALONE IN THE
MORNING.
THE FISH IS GONE
THAT IS GREAT
BACK TO THE WAY
THINGS NEED TO BE
EVERYTHING IS RIGHT
I'LL JUST SIT TIGHT
ONE MORE NIGHT
TILL THE MORNING
YES, FINE,
EVERYTHING IS FINE.
YES, FINE,
DEFINITELY FINE
YES, FINE,
POSITIVELY FINE
NOTHING HAS CHANGED
IT'S ALL THE SAME
YES
THINK IT SHOULD BE FINE
EVERYTHING WILL BE
EVERYTHING SHOULD BE
EVERYTHING CAN BE
EVERYTHING IS FINE!

Act 3

Scene 1

Rosaleen *appears, holding a sparkly gift box.*

Rosaleen   Bart.

Bart   Mother.

Rosaleen   What did I say about calling me Mother?

Bart   Well you are my mother, aren't you? Unless there's another curve ball coming my way today.

Rosaleen   Where's Harvey?

Bart   We had an argument.

Rosaleen   About what?

Bart   A goldfish.

Rosaleen   Oh?

Bart   It landed on our doorstep, out of the blue.

Rosaleen   Right.

Bart   Harvey said he loves it. And . . . I don't get it. What is there to love? Anyway, it's gone now.

Rosaleen   Where?

Bart   To a pet shelter.

Beat.

Harvey will be home soon.

Rosaleen   What makes you so sure? I didn't go home.

Bart   What do you mean?

Rosaleen   To your father.

Bart   Why do you keep talking about him? First at my anniversary party, and now here.

Rosaleen   You don't recognise any of this behaviour?

Bart   What behaviour?

Rosaleen   Rejecting something outright, before you've even tried to understand it. Not seeing the value in it. Pushing away the ones who love you the most.

Bart   No, I do not.

Roslaeen   Bart, look at what you're doing.

Bart   I'm not doing anything. It's everyone else that's doing things. Sandra leaving. Harvey deciding to be in love with this fish.

Rosaleen   Everyone else is the problem, are they?

Bart   Yes, now you understand.

Rosaleen   Why don't you go and find Harvey?

Bart   I am not going anywhere. I'm staying right here. He'll come back. They'll all come back.

Rosaleen   Well looks like I'm right on time.

Rosaleen *hands him the gift.*

Bart   What's this?

Rosaleen   You seemed disappointed that I didn't bring a proper gift to your anniversary party, so . . .

Bart   Oh! Thank you.

Bart *opens the box. Turns it upside down . . . nothing.*

Em . . . What is it?

Rosaleen   It's a story.

Bart   Wow, first advice and now a story. I wonder what I'll get for Christmas – a metaphor?

Rosaleen   Once upon a time a very beautiful, witty woman with phenomenal legs met a man and they fell in love.

Bart   Wow.

Rosaleen   This woman couldn't believe her luck, the man was perfect. Tall, handsome and he had a few bob, which always helps. They got married and had a baby boy. Life was complete, they had everything they ever wanted.

Over time they realised that their little boy was different to the other boys. He had a skip in his step, a swish in his hip – he caught the light, he sparkled.

Bart   A swish in his hip?

Rosaleen   The little boy's father didn't like who his son was becoming. He was afraid. And so, he told his son to stop being so fabulous. He said no. And when the boy's mother picked him up, packed their bags and took him away, the man did nothing. He –

Bart   Stop. That is enough. (*beat*) I'd like to return this gift – it's annoying me.

Rosaleen *sighs a decades-long sigh*.

Song. The Little Things.

Rosaleen   IT'S THE LITTLE THINGS
                     I LET FLY
                     THAT I REGRET THE MOST

                     THE TUT HE MADE
                     HOW HE BEHAVED
                     HIS EYES WHEN HE SAID NO

Bart   OH, HERE WE GO AGAIN

Rosaleen	FUNNY HOW LITTLE THINGS REPEAT THEMSELVES LIKE FATHER, LIKE SON
	SOMETHING NEW OUT OF THE BLUE SURPRISES EVERYONE
	I THOUGHT YOU AND ALL YOU'VE BEEN THROUGH MIGHT NOT DO WHAT HE'S DONE
	BUT, HERE WE GO AGAIN
Bart	YOU'RE COMPARING ME TO HIM?
Rosaleen	I'M JUST SAYING WHAT I SEE
Bart	THAT MAN PUSHED US OUT
Rosaleen	WHERE'S THE FISH, WHERE'S HARVEY?
Bart	THIS IS A LITTLE THING –
Rosaleen	THAT I WILL NOT LET FLY I SEE WHAT YOU'RE DOING SO HERE I GO AGAIN!
	I SEE THE LITTLE THINGS YOUR TONE WHEN YOU SAY NO I SEE THE LITTLE THINGS YOU SHUT DOWN WHAT YOU CAN'T CONTROL
	I SEE A LITTLE BOY
Bart	THAT IS ALWAYS AFRAID
Rosaleen	A LITTLE BOY
Bart	WHOSE DAD SAID NO!

Rosaleen	I SEE A LITTLE BOY
Bart	WHO NEEDS TO FEEL SAFE
Both	A LITTLE BOY INSIDE A FRIGHTENED MAN WHO CAN'T HANDLE CHANGE
	I NEED HARVEY BACK AGAIN
Rosaleen	BUT HARVEY'S ASKING YOU TO CHANGE
Bart	AND IF I DON'T, AND IF I CAN'T?
Rosaleen	THEN DON'T EXPECT HIM TO STAY
Bart	WHAT WILL I DO?
Rosaleen	IT'S NOT A LITTLE THING TO SHOW HIM YOU HEAR HIM IT'S NOT A LITTLE THING TO TRY SOMETHING NEW IT'S NOT A LITTLE THING TO FIND HIM AND TELL HIM THAT GOLDEN LITTLE THING IS WELCOME HERE WITH YOU
Bart	ANYTHING FOR HARVEY
Rosaleen	A LITTLE THING
Bart	ANYTHING AT ALL
Rosaleen	THAT'S MY BOY
Bart	ANYTHING HE NEEDS FROM ME
Both	ANY LITTLE THING CAN REALLY CHANGE IT ALL BIG OR SMALL

Bart *runs off to do . . . something.* **Rosaleen** *picks up her gift, turns out it wasn't such a bad one after all.*

Scene 2

*A **Mouse** rushes forward as Pet'Ernal Love Pet Shelter forms around her.*

Song. Manic Mouse.

Mouse	HIYA HIYA,
	I'M A MOUSE
	WOULD YOU LIKE
	A PET MOUSE?

I KNOW, I KNOW
WHY PICK A MOUSE
WE LIVE FOR FREE
UNDER YOUR HOUSE.

YOU KNOW THE
SAYING CAT'S AWAY
LET'S HAVE FUN
I LOVE TO PLAY

SORRY I JUST
GOT A FRIGHT
IT'S QUITE SPOOKY
HERE AT NIGHT

I HAVE DREAMED OF
ROAMING FREE
IN THE FIELDS
AND THROUGH THE TREES

RACING ROUND
WITH OTHER MICE
SCARING PEOPLE
IN THE NIGHT

BUT I KNOW
THAT CAN'T COME TRUE
INSTEAD I'LL GO
HOME WITH YOU

I NEED A HOME
YOU HAVE A HOME
I'M SUPER FUN
BRING ME HOME

I NEED A HOME
YOU HAVE A HOME
I'M SUPER FUN
BRING ME HOME

I NEED A HOME
YOU HAVE A HOME
I'M SUPER FUN
BRING ME HOME

BRING ME HOME

All   HEY TAKE US HOME
TO LIVE WITH YOU
WE'RE HOPING OUR
DAYS HERE ARE THROUGH

HEY TAKE US HOME
TO LIVE WITH YOU
IT'S TIME TO GO
FROM THIS REFUGE

AND WHAT YOU GET
YES, IN RETURN
IS THAT WITH US
YOU'RE NOT ALONE!

COME PICK US UP
AND BRING US HOME . . .

Mouse   HIYA HIYA
WANT A MOUSE?
I'LL BE SO FUN
IN YOUR HOUSE!

I'M FUN I SWEAR
I'M PRETTY CUTE

TAKE ME WITH YOU
I'M A HOOT

I NEED TO GO
I NEED TO GO
PICK ME QUICKLY
BRING ME HOME

BRING ME HOME

I NEED TO GO
I NEED TO GO
PICK ME QUICKLY
BRING ME HOME

BRING ME HOME

All   WE NEED TO GO
WE NEED TO GO
PICK ME QUICKLY
BRING ME HOME

BRING ME HOME

WE NEED TO GO
WE NEED TO GO
PICK ME QUICKLY
BRING ME HOME

BRING ME –

Silence. The **PSO** *enters, furious. She displays the* **Goldfish** *in the bowl.*

PSO   Yes! Your eyes do not betray you. This fish is indeed in a bowl. A bowl! A bowl. A . . . bowl. This is the final straw. What I need to do now is clear.

The **PSO** *takes the phone off the hook – ding. The pets are spooked.*

I'm locking the door. Lowering the blinds. None of you, not one of you, will ever leave this place again.

The pets are freaked.

None of you, not one of you will ever suffer another human, another home, another hell in your lifetime. You'll live out your lives and die here, with me. Here we'll all be safe. None of us, not one of us, will ever leave here ever again.

Cockatoo   Ever leave here again?

PSO   Yes. Here with me, you'll forever be safe.

Cockatoo   Forever?

PSO   Indeed, worth repeating. Forever! We'll never, ever leave!

Cockatoo   Never ever leave?

The pets are panicking.

PSO   Oh . . . I know what you're thinking – what about me? Will I not miss humanity, my brethren, my kind? Absolutely not. What about the demands on my body, I hear you shriek? The physical strain that comes with all of this care – the calluses, the fleas, the unexplained infections? Rest assured, my feathered and furry friends, my reward is all of you. As my father used to say –

Song. Never Quite Alone.

YOU ARE NEVER QUITE ALONE
WITH A PET
YOU ARE NEVER QUITE ALONE.

WHEN THERE'S NO ONE AT ALL
AND THE WORLD FEELS SMALL
NO, I WON'T BE UPSET
I HAVE STILL GOT MY PETS

RABBIT YOU'RE ADORABLE
SAFE IN HERE WITH ME
NO CHANCE OF FALLING FOUL
OF ANY MALE COMPANY

*The **Rabbit** turns away.*

> WHEN THERE'S NO ONE AT ALL
> AND THE WORLD FEELS VERY
> SMALL
> ALTHOUGH I'D LOVE A DUET
> I'M NOT SOLO WITH YOU PETS

All
> YOU ARE NEVER QUITE ALONE
> WITH A PET
> YOU ARE NEVER QUITE ALONE.
>
> COCKATOO YOU DON'T SAY
> MUCH
> I HAVEN'T HEARD BEFORE
> YOU LOVE THE SOUND OF MY
> SWEET VOICE
> YOU DON'T NEED ANY MORE

*The **Cockatoo** turns away.*

> LITTLE GOLDFISH
> YOU'RE SAFE NOW
> FROM THOSE AWFUL MEN
> I'LL MAKE SURE THAT YOU
> NEVER
> HAVE TO LIVE WITH THEM
> AGAIN

*The **Goldfish** flickers and dims.*

> WHEN THERE'S NO ONE AT ALL
> AND THE WORLD FEELS SMALL
> WHEN I'M FEELING UPSET
> I'M NOT ALONE, I'VE GOT PETS
>
> ALL I'M ASKING IN RETURN
> IS THAT YOU STAY WITH ME
> I'LL KEEP YOU SAFE AND SOUND
> AND YOU'LL KEEP ME COMPANY

SHOW ME YOU CAN HEAR ME
TELL ME THAT YOU AGREE
LET ME KNOW YOU'RE ALL ON
BOARD
THAT YOU'RE HAPPY HERE WITH
ME

YOU ARE NEVER QUITE ALONE
WITH A PET
YOU ARE NEVER –

All of the pets have turned away.

WHY DO YOU TURN AWAY?
DO YOU HAVE SOMETHING TO
SAY
WHY ARE YOU ALL SO SAD?
DID I DO SOMETHING BAD?

The **PSO** *looks at the* **Goldfish**, *flickering in despair.*

PLEASE TELL ME
WHAT CAN'T I SEE
ARE YOU UPSET
'CAUSE OF ME?

Scene 3

Harvey *and* **Deirdre** *are at* **Deirdre***'s place.* **Deirdre** *is putting on a pencil outfit.*

Deirdre   Will you help me into this?

Harvey   Why a pencil?

Deirdre   I'm entertaining at a literacy party this morning, celebrating a kid being able to write.

Harvey   Oh.

Deirdre   2B or not 2B, that is the question!

Harvey (*sadly*)   Funny.

Deirdre   Eraser, I hardly know her.

Harvey   Good one.

Deirdre (*under her breath*)   Well, that went down like a lead balloon.

Harvey   Thanks for letting me stay the night.

Deirdre   Any time, pal. My fold-out mattress will always have your name on it.

Harvey   I might need it. I don't know if I want to go home. Bart was so angry, I've never seen him like that. It was awful. He hurt my feelings.

Deirdre   Ugh, feelings. So tricky.

Harvey   And Fishy is gone now, too.

Deirdre   Which is a relief.

Harvey   What?

Deirdre   That's what you wanted, right?

Harvey   No. Before yesterday morning I never thought about having a fish. But now I can't imagine my life without it.

Deirdre   What?

Harvey   That's what Bart and I had an argument about. Actually, before the pet shelter owner came to our house everything was going really well.

Beat.

Deirdre   Huh.

Harvey   Huh what?

Deirdre   Em. I can't help but feel that I might be a tiny bit responsible for all this.

Harvey   Why?

Deirdre   I may have gone to the pet shelter and told the pet shelter owner that you and Bart were psychopathic monsters who were torturing the goldfish, determined to kill it and turn it into sushi. Then gave her your address.

Harvey   What?

Deirdre   I thought that's what you wanted. Remember 'asking for a friend'?

Harvey   Yeah.

Deirdre   Didn't your 'friend' want to get rid of the fish? (*winky face*)

Harvey   No!

Deirdre   Oh, right.

Harvey   That is the opposite of what I wanted.

Deirdre   Okay. Maybe my little 'asking for a friend' trick isn't a great idea after all. Probably best to just be direct in future.

Harvey   Why would you do that, Deirdre?

Song. Asking for a Friend (*reprise*).

Deirdre

I DON'T KNOW WHY
I DO ANYTHING?
THAT'S THE TRUTH.

I . . .
AM . . .
A . . .
PENCIL
A CARROT
A WEATHER SYSTEM
SOMETIMES A PARROT

I . . .
HAVE . . .
NO IDEA
WHO I AM

Deirdre *has a momentary existential panic.*

I'VE GOT A FRIEND
MADE A MISTAKE
SHE DIDN'T MEAN TO
SHE JUST GOT CONFUSED
SHOULD SHE SAY SORRY?
OR SHOULD SHE RUN AWAY?

Harvey   Deirdre, it's okay.

Deirdre

NO NO IT'S NOT COZ
SHE FEELS REALLY BAD
AND EXISTENTIALLY
CHALLENGED
IS SHE A FRIEND AT ALL?

Harvey   Deirdre, stop asking for a friend. I know you're talking about yourself.

Deirdre   Okay.

Harvey   You're the best friend ever. You just need to say sorry.

Deirdre   Sorry.

Harvey   There, that's it sorted.

Deirdre   No, now I need to fix things for you.

> I HAVE DONE IT AGAIN
> NOW LET ME RACK MY BRAIN
> WHAT'S THE PERFECT WAY
> TO FIX THIS MESSED-UP GAME
> LET'S SEE MY FRIEND
> CAN I MAKE AMENDS?
> AND BRING THIS SITUATION TO
> AN END
> I'LL JUST BE CLEAR AND TELL
> BART I MESSED THINGS UP

Harvey   Okay!

Both
> TURNS OUT THAT BEING CLEAR
> IS PROBABLY ENOUGH
> BEING DIRECT IT SEEMS IS JUST
> EASIER
> AND COMES WITH FAR LESS FEAR
> I'LL JUST BE SINCERE

Both
> IF YOU'RE AFRAID
> DON'T ASK FOR A FRIEND
> THAT'S NOT A GREAT IDEA
> IT GETS MESSY IN THE END
> SOMETHING YOU CAN'T SAY
> JUST BE HONEST AND TRUE

Deirdre
> I'LL FIX THIS
> FOR YOU MY FRIEND.

Scene 4

Bart *is rushing to go and get* **Harvey** *back. He bumps into* **Sandra**.

Sandra   Oh. Hi.

Bart   Hi.

Sandra   Em.

Bart   Yeah.

Sandra   This is a bit awkward, is it?

Bart   No. I'm not. Awkward.

Sandra   Okay. I went through the boxes and found some glass glue. I thought you could use it to fix the fish tank.

Bart   That's kind of you, but I don't need it anymore.

Sandra   Did you fix it?

Bart   No, I threw it away. And then a very angry woman invaded our house and took the fish away. And then Harvey and I had an argument. He stayed at Deirdre's house, and I'm on my way to find him and apologise.

Sandra   That's a lot of things. Why didn't you call me?

Bart   I –

Sandra   You always call me when things like this happen.

Bart   Well, you're busy. You've got the babies and the move . . . I didn't want to bother you.

Sandra   Bother me!? Bart, that makes me so angry.

Bart   Angry?

Bart *starts to cry.*

Sandra   Are you crying?

Bart   Yeah, ignore me. I just had a big moment with my mum and . . . it dragged up some stuff about my dad and . . . things I've I lost out on and . . . some feelings I've been really pushing down for the last couple of decades, but. . . this isn't about me, go on – you were saying I made you angry.

Sandra   Crying in my face really makes it hard for me to follow through on the anger, **Bart**.

Bart (*He stops crying*)   Please, go ahead.

Sandra   I'm angry because when I told you we were moving yesterday, you didn't say anything. Even though I know you were upset. You acted like you didn't care at all. Why didn't you cry then?

Bart *cries again.*

Bart   Why didn't you tell me you were leaving?

Sandra   Honestly?

Bart   Yes.

Sandra   Because I was afraid of upsetting you.

Bart   Everyone is so afraid of upsetting me.

Bart *cries a little more.*

Sandra   Bart, the crying is a bit triggering – I spend 90% of my time around crying babies.

Bart   Sorry, I'll stop.

Sandra   I'm really nervous about moving, Bart. I'm moving away from everything that I know, and all the people that I love. I feel like I'm starting all over again. And I need you to be there for me. I need my best friend.

Bart *has a little whimper.* **Sandra** *gestures at him not to start crying again.*

Sandra   So, that means I can't be worried about telling you things in case they might upset you.

Bart   Okay. Sorry.

Sandra   And let's be clear about something – you didn't lose out on anything, Bart. Your father did. An amazing little boy landed into his life from out of the blue. And because of how that man behaved, he lost out on the most important person in my life. My best friend.

Bart   Thanks.

Beat.

Sandra   That didn't make you cry?

Bart *shrugs*.

Sandra   Right, enough of this. Go get Harvey.

Bart   I love you pal.

Sandra   Love you too.

Deirdre *rushes in*.

Deirdre   Hiya Sandra.

Sandra   A pencil, nice.

Deirdre   Bart, this is all my fault. In a very convoluted series of events that were all entirely unprecedented and unexpected I went to the pet shelter dressed as a weather system and told that woman that you and Harvey were blowtorching the mysterious goldfish that landed on your doorstep. It turns out that was not the right thing to do, and that it may have had a negative impact on your relationship with Harvey. And for that, I am sorry.

Sandra   Deirdre, you are incredibly odd.

Bart   Never change.

Deirdre   I'm actually perpetually changing, and I'm okay with that. Change is a good thing, Bart. It's a little uncomfortable and can be a bit provocative emotionally, but it's good. Without change you'd just be an egg sitting on your own letting your soupy insides harden into a congealed stasis, which would eventually start to smell and bother other people.

Bart   Okay.

Deirdre   Right, that's as far as my peace and reconciliation skills go. Just wanted to get all that out of the way before . . .

Harvey *enters.*

Deirdre   We'll leave you to it.

Sandra   Yep.

Deirdre   We'll just listen at the door.

Sandra *and* **Deirdre** *leave.*

Bart   Harvey.

Harvey   Yes Bart.

Bart   I am so sorry.

Harvey   Okay.

Bart   For all of it. For not listening to you. For rejecting the fish. For saying no. This isn't your fault, you haven't done anything wrong. It was me, I was rejecting things that made me uncomfortable. I'm going to try really hard not to do that anymore.

Harvey   Mm.

Bart   There is no one that I can think of who is better equipped to care for another living thing than you.

Harvey   You were really mean.

Bart   I was. I'm sorry.

Harvey   How sorry?

Bart   What?

Harvey   How sorry are you?

Bart   Like, do you want me to quantify it?

Harvey   Yes.

Bart   Em.

Harvey   Or, if that's too difficult for you. You could *do* something to show me how sorry you are.

Bart   Anything.

Harvey   Bark.

Bart   What?

Harvey   Bark like a dog.

Bart   Woof.

Harvey   You don't seem like a very sorry dog.

Bart (*like a sorry dog*)   Woof.

Harvey   I've never met a dog that stands on two legs before.

Bart (*down on all fours*)   Woof, woof.

Harvey   Are you a sorry dog?

Bart   Woof.

Harvey   Where's the paw?

Bart *gives the paw.*

Harvey   Bang bang.

Bart *rolls over.*

Harvey (*rubbing his belly*)   Best little doggy. I forgive you.

Bart   Harvey, I love you so much. If you really want a pet in the house I'm happy to stay being a dog.

Harvey   No thanks, I'm more of a fish person.

Bart   I know. Me too.

Song. Come back. Come Home.

Bart	I NEVER THOUGHT I'D SAY THIS BUT I AM REALLY SAD
Harvey	THESE ARE THE SADDEST FEELINGS THAT I HAVE EVER HAD.
Bart	I DIDN'T GIVE THE FISH A CHANCE ITS TINY LITTLE FACE.
Harvey	I MISS THE FISH SO MUCH JUST SWIMMING ROUND THE PLACE.
Bart	I'M SORRY I CALLED THE FISH A PAIN. I WILL NEVER PUSH YOU AWAY AGAIN.
Harvey	I'D GIVE ANYTHING TO BRING OUR LITTLE FISHY HOME IF ONLY WE DIDN'T PUT IT IN A CRYSTAL BOWL.
Bart	YOU'RE GONE.
Harvey	YOU'RE GONE.
Both	WE'LL MISS THE THINGS YOU DO. WE'LL NEVER EVER HAVE YOU BACK AGAIN.
Harvey	YOU'RE GONE.
Bart	AWAY.
Both	AND WE WILL BOTH MISS YOU WE'RE LOST AND WE JUST DON'T KNOW WHAT TO DO?

Harvey   You know, I'd landed on a great name for the fish.

Bart   Oh?

Harvey   Glenda, it's a combination of Brenda and Glen.

Bart   Very imaginative. But I think I prefer Fishy.

Harvey   Yeah, me too.

Bart	I WISH WE HAD MORE TIME FOR FISHY, ME AND YOU.
Harvey	THE HOUSE FEELS SO EMPTY WITH JUST US LONELY TWO.
Bart	I DIDN'T KNOW THE JOY OF SEEING FISHY SWIM.
Harvey	WE NEVER REALLY KNEW IF IT WAS HER OR THEM OR HIM.
Bart	I'M SORRY I CALLED THE FISH A PAIN. I WILL NEVER PUSH YOU AWAY AGAIN.
Harvey	I'D GIVE ANYTHING TO BRING OUR LITTLE FISHY HOME
Bart	I CAN'T BELIEVE SHE TOOK FISHY DAMN HER HEART OF STONE.

Sandra, **Tom**, **Rosaleen** and **Deirdre** *enter*.

All	COME BACK. COME HOME. WE MISS THE THINGS YOU DO. OUR LIVES WILL NEVER EVER BE THE SAME. COME BACK. COME HOME. WE LOVE YOU

THROUGH AND THROUGH
WE'LL NEVER HAVE YOU BACK
WITH US AGAIN

Bart & Harvey   WE'LL NEVER HAVE YOU BACK

WITH US AGAIN

Pause.

Tom   So, that's it? You're just going to give up?

Bart   Yes, it's over.

Harvey   We made a mistake.

Bart   We were wrong.

Tom   No, no, no, no, no, no, no. It's not over!

Deirdre   You weren't wrong!

Bart   No, we were.

Harvey   The pet shelter owner said we were.

Bart   The fish almost died.

Tom   Almost died, yes. But was it actually dead?

Bart   Em . . .

Harvey   No.

Tom   Then what's the problem?

Sandra   If we just gave up every time our children *nearly* died then we'd have been out of the game months ago.

Deirdre   You know, when I was a child I was always nearly dead. My entire childhood was spent on the brink of death. Death was my best friend. Death was my only friend. I was first in line to die all the time, but someone kept skipping me in the queue.

Rosaleen   I feel very uncomfortable.

Deirdre   I didn't give up. I fought the fires, I stopped playing with the knives, I remembered no hair dryers near the bath and I was absolutely fine.

Rosaleen   This woman works with children?

Sandra   The truth is everyone's child is constantly on the brink of death. That's what being alive is.

Tom   And our job, as the bigger people taking care of the smaller ones, is to see that brink and do something. Moment by moment. There is no right and wrong, there's no road map, there's no book to read.

Rosaleen   There are actually loads of books to read.

Tom   I'm not a big reader Rosaleen. And anyway, books don't raise children, people do!

Sandra   There's no training, there's no practice.

Tom   You're in the hot seat, blindly trying to fight off death.

Deirdre   Until finally it comes to take one or both of you.

                     Song. Don't give up.

Tom   THERE WAS ONE TIME
                               ON MY BED,
                               I WAS CHANGING MY BABY'S
                               NAPPY
                               THEN I GOT
                               DISTRACTED BY SOMETHING
                               FLAPPY
                               AND HE ROLLED OFF THE BED

                               HE FELL ON HIS HEAD.
                               AND HE CRIED
                               THEN HE STOPPED CRYING
                               AND IT WAS SILENT

AND I THOUGHT . . .
OH DEAR . . .
AND THEN HE CRIED AGAIN
AND I THOUGHT GREAT!
HE'S NOT DEAD,
HE JUST FELL ON HIS HEAD

All
HE'S NOT DEAD,
HE JUST FELL ON HIS HEAD!
HE'S NOT DEAD
HE JUST FELL
HE JUST FELL
ON HIS HEAD

Rosaleen
CAN I SHARE SOMETHING?
I'M SCARED OF BUYING GIFTS
SINCE BART'S TENTH BIRTHDAY
YOU SEE I BOUGHT HIM
AN ELECTRIC GUITAR

HE PLUGGED THE THING IN
TO A PORT NEAR THE SINK
GOT A SHOCK AND PASSED OUT
AND THEY HAD TO RESTART HIS
HEART!

Bart   What!?

Sandra
I BURNED MY
SON'S HAND WITH A PAN ONCE.
I FORGOT MY TWO DAUGHTERS
IN A TROLLEY AT THE STORE
BUT I TURNED RIGHT ROUND
AND COLLECTED THEM

All
KEEP ON GOING
UNTIL YOU'RE DEAD
KEEP ON FIGHTING
UNTIL THE END
AND IF YOU ARE NOT DEAD
THEN YOU'RE LIVING!

KEEP ON GOING
UNTIL YOU'RE GONE
DON'T STOP FAILING
JUST CARRY ON
SO DON'T YOU GIVE UP
KEEP ON LIVING!

Deirdre   I ASKED MY MUM
IF SHE DROPPED ME
AND SHE SAID YES ALL THE TIME
AND I'M FINE!

Tom   ONE TIME MY FATHER
BROKE MY ANKLE
WHEN HE FORCED MY CHUNKY
FEET INTO MY SHOES

Bart & Harvey   WE BURST THE BAG
THE FISH WAS IN
AND PUT IT IN OUR MOUTHS
AND SPAT IT OUT
INTO A BOWL
AND FED IT CHEMICALS.

Baby 1   WAAAAAAAAAA
WAAAAAAAAAA

All   AWWWWWWW

Tom   BECAUSE LIFE IS WORTH LIVING

All   LET'S KEEP ON LIVING

Sandra   I WON'T GIVE UP UNTIL
I'M DEAD

All   AND IF THERE'S SOMETHING
OR SOMEONE
THAT MEANS THE WORLD TO
YOU
A DAUGHTER OR A SON
OR A FISH OR A MAN

THEN DO EVERYTHING
YOU POSSIBLY CAN
DON'T GIVE UP ON THEM
DON'T GIVE UP

All KEEP ON GOING
UNTIL YOU'RE DEAD
KEEP ON FIGHTING
UNTIL THE END
AND IF YOU ARE NOT DEAD
THEN YOU'RE LIVING!
KEEP ON GOING
UNTIL YOU'RE DEAD
KEEP ON FIGHTING
UNTIL THE END
SO DON'T YOU GIVE UP
KEEP ON LIVING!

Deirdre I MAKE SO MANY MISTAKES

Tom I HAVE NO CLUE WHAT I'M
DOING

Sandra I WRITE OFF WHOLE DAYS AS A
FAILURE

All DON'T GIVE UP
DON'T GIVE UP
DON'T GIVE UP
DON'T GIVE UP
DON'T GIVE UP
DON'T GIVE UP
DON'T GIVE UP
DON'T GIVE UP

Bart & Harvey WON'T GIVE UP
WON'T GIVE UP
NO NOT US

All DON'T GIVE UP!

Scene 5

The **PSO** *appears.*

PSO   Hello again. From your facial expressions I gather that you're surprised to see me.

Harvey   Have you come back to shout at us again?

Bart   Because this time we're prepared to shout back!

Bart, **Harvey** *and their friends shout at the* **PSO** *like a bawdy rabble. The* **PSO** *gestures to stop, and they all freeze into silence.*

PSO   I am here to do my job. To provide refuge for a goldfish in need of a home.

Harvey   Fishy!

PSO   What was that?

Bart   Fishy, it's the name we gave the goldfish.

Harvey   Our goldfish.

PSO   Slightly unimaginative, but not harmful to the fish, so I'll let it slide. Last night I brought the fish back to my shelter and flushed all the chemicals out of its system. I swore to provide a home for this fish until it sucked its final molecules of oxygen from the water around it.

Bart   That's very specific.

PSO   However, it appears that I am not what this fish needs. Whilst the two of you broke the rules, made idiotic mistakes and put the fish in great danger – you did not reject it.

Bart   I did, in fact, reject it, however, I've grown since then and now wholeheartedly accept it.

PSO   I will never stand in the way of what a pet needs. And what this fish needs is you.

She holds out the **Goldfish**.

You are its family.

Bart & Harvey   Fishy!

PSO   Wait. As you can see, I have provided you with another tank. I have also thrown in a comprehensive pamphlet on fish care, free of charge.

Bart   How very kind of you.

Harvey   Free pamphlet!

Bart   This is all quite a surprise. To be honest, we were on our way to your shelter for what was shaping up to be an epic and passionate battle.

Harvey   Our friend dropped his baby on his head but his reluctance to give up in the face of near-fatal error really inspired us.

Tom   It'd be *super* if we didn't keep repeating that.

Bart   It's actually quite convenient that you changed your mind.

PSO   I didn't change my mind. The fish and the other pets, they changed my mind. I run a shelter, but what they want is . . . a home. So, here.

Harvey *takes the* **Goldfish** *back*.

PSO (*concerned for the pet*)   This fish is depending on you. Promise me that you'll take care of it.

Harvey   Absolutely.

Bart   We promise.

An awkward pause.

PSO   I'm going to need to charge you for the tank this time.

Bart   Oh!

PSO   I'm not made of tanks.

Bart   Of course.

PSO   Cash or card?

Bart (**Bart** *pays her.*)   Oh, cash. Here.

PSO   Well, that completes our transaction. I'll hit the road.

Harvey   Wait! What about you?

PSO   Me?

Bart   Where is your home?

Harvey   Who are your people?

PSO   I'm not much of a people person.

Harvey   Well, why don't you stay?

Bart   Yeah, join us.

Harvey   I could brush your hair, if you like?

PSO   How nice, but no.

Bart   Are you sure? We'd love to have you.

Both   You'd be super welcome.

PSO   Oh, wow. Sorry . . . feeling a feeling. Em, maybe some other time.

Bart   Okay then.

Harvey   Thank you for bringing Fishy back to us.

PSO   Okay. Good luck.

The **PSO** *exits.* **Bart & Harvey** *burst into an outpouring of love for the fish, fawning and cooing.*

Bart (*as if talking to a baby*)   Oh Fishy / wishy! Oh I'm so sorry about the chemical poisoning. Oh, I made such a big boo boo. You little trooper-wooper, you made it.

Harvey (*as if talking to a baby*)   Oh, you're home again you little scaly scamp! Oh I love you so much. You slippery little bean. Oh, who's the best little fishy wishy.

Sandra   Alright. It's time for us to go.

Tom   Yep. The moving van charges by the hour.

Deirdre   I've to head off, too. I've got a gender reveal party tonight and I'm going dressed in green. That'll confuse the crap out of them.

Rosaleen   I'll go too, for no other reason but that I feel a little awkward.

Sandra   This feels like the end of something.

Deirdre   Dramatic.

Harvey   But the start of something too.

Bart   Yeah, the start of something new.

Rosaleen   Right, that's my cue. I'm not one for emotional goodbyes. I'm not one for emotions at all, in fact. Easier that way.

Bart (*going to hug* **Rosaleen**)   Thanks for everything, Mum.

Rosaleen   Nope, still not a hugger. But yes, you can call me 'Mum'.

Rosaleen *exits.*

Bart   Some things do change.

Sandra   And some things will never change.

Deirdre   And some change will change the changey-change.

Sandra, Tom & Deirdre   Bye boys.

Bart & Harvey   Bye.

Sandra *and* **Tom** *and* **Deirdre** *leave.* **Bart** *and* **Harvey** *are alone again with the* **Goldfish**.

Bart   Do you think Fishy is hungry?

Harvey   Maybe.

Bart *gets the fish food.*

Bart   This is the food, right?

Harvey   Yes.

Bart   How much do we sprinkle in?

Harvey   Let me check the pamphlet. (*He checks the pamphlet*) One pinch.

Song. Start Again.

Bart	TIME TO MAKE A CHANGE DO SOMETHING NEW
Harvey	LET'S START AGAIN FROM THE BEGINNING
Both	WE CAN START AGAIN TAKE IT FROM THE TOP NO NEED TO FREAK OUT IF WE MESS THINGS UP START AGAIN AND LET SOMETHING NEW OUT OF THE BLUE TRANSFORM YOU START AGAIN JUMP IN THE DEEP END

START AGAIN
DON'T WEAR ARM BANDS

All of the characters return to the stage and join **Bart** *and* **Harvey**.

All   A FRESH PERSPECTIVE
                       A NEW POINT OF VIEW
                       AN ALTERNATIVE METHOD
                       DO SOMETHING NEW

PSO   EVERY DAY IS A CHANCE TO
                       START AGAIN

All   WE CAN START
                       OVER AND OVER
                       AND OVER
                       AND OVER
                       AND START AGAIN
                       EVERY DAY
                       FIND SOMETHING NEW
                       START AGAIN
                       DON'T EVER GIVE UP
                       DO SOMETHING NEW
                       START AGAIN
                       IT'S OKAY
                       LET THE PAST GO
                       START AGAIN
                       IT'S NEVER TOO LATE
                       DO SOMETHING NEW

The **Cockatoo** *emerges, and takes her place – like at the beginning.*

                       START AGAIN
                       YOU'RE HUMAN
                       DON'T BE AFRAID TO FAIL
                       START AGAIN
                       IT'S NEVER TOO LATE
                       BLAZE A BRAND NEW TRAIL
                       START AGAIN

IT'S WORTH IT
DON'T YOU EVER GIVE UP
START AGAIN
AND OPEN YOUR HEART
IT'S OKAY TO START
TO START OVER AGAIN

Cockatoo   SOMETHING NEW
OUT OF THE BLUE
JUST LANDS RIGHT IN
ON TOP OF YOU
WELL
WHAT DO YOU DO?

All   SOMETHING NEW

A new **Goldfish** *descends from the cosmos, and this time lands in* **Deirdre**'s *hands. Gasp!*

End of Play.